# THE 350TH FIGHTER GROUP

## IN THE MEDITERRANEAN CAMPAIGN
## 2 November 1942 to 2 May 1945

**Schiffer Military History**
Atglen, PA

*The 350th Fighter Group was formed on 1 October 1942, with headquarters in Great Britain. The first fliers had already seen action with other U. S. Groups, or had been members of the Royal Air Force or Royal Canadian Air Force. Meanwhile the ground crews were training in the United States. By January 1943, the Group was together and elements had entered into combat operations in North Africa. The Group insignia is blue on the left, suggesting Great Britain, surmounted with a suggestion of Royal Air Force Wings, the gold on the right suggesting America, surmounted with a suggestion of U.S.A.A.F. Wings and the brown band surmounted by an Arabic motto suggesting North Africa The meaning of the Arabic is "Boldness and Vigor". Above this are seven stars for battle participation in seven campaigns.*

**Cover artwork by Steve Ferguson, Colorado Springs, CO.**

**KNIGHT'S QUEST**

Lt. Raymond Knight was a driven warrior, absolutely fearless and totally confident of his mission. The 346th Fighter Squadron flight leader would take his P-47 strafers into the gates of hell to destroy the Luftwaffe and proved it sortie after sortie. By April 1945 the Allies were poised to cross the Po River and liberate Milan, an objective only minutes from the 350th FG base at Pisa. Weather permitting, Knight was at times able to fly three missions per day in his pursuit of the last of the Luftwaffe. He completely wore out one aircraft in the quest and had only recently acquired his latest P-47 from a Spanish squadron. Seeing the lastest photo reconnaissance of the landing fields at Bergamo and Ghedi, he led many sorties there in his refit "OH JOHNNIE" for two days running. Purportedly responsible for at least twenty aircraft personally destroyed, the lieutenant was determined to find more. In the morning twilight of April 25, 1945, Knight swept in over Bergamo airdrome attempting to eliminate the last enemy planes hidden there. He was immediately bracketed by the withering crossfire of antiaircraft guns surrounding the field and barely escaped to the south in his riddled Thunderbolt. He opted to try Pisa, but the turbulence over the Appenine Mountains was too severe for his war torn plane. As JOHNNIE snap rolled and plummeted earthward, Knight attempted to bail out but was much too low. Lt. Raymond Knight was awarded a posthumous Medal of Honor, the last airman to be so honored for conspicuous bravery in the European theatre.

Copyright © 1997 by Schiffer Publishing Ltd.
Library of Congress Catalog Number: 96-70842.

Printed in the United States of America.
ISBN: 0-7643-0220-5

We are interested in hearing from authors with book ideas on related topics.

Published by Schiffer Publishing Ltd.
77 Lower Valley Road
Atglen, PA 19310
Phone: (610) 593-1777
FAX: (610) 593-2002
Please write for a free catalog.
This book may be purchased from the publisher.
Please include $2.95 postage.
Try your bookstore first.

350 TH FIGHTER GROUP

# MAJOR GENERAL CHIDLAW ACCEPTS THE SURRE[

These historic photographs, made at Headquarters, 12th Air Force, show the final humiliation of the Luftwaffe in the Mediterranean. Major General Benjamin W. Chidlaw explains the terms of surrender to Colonel Frederich Wollbracht, the central figure on the right.

Longer than any other U.S.A.A.F. Group, the 350th Fighter Group stood guard against the Luftwaffe over the troopships, merchantmen and warships of the Allied Nations plying the Mediterranean. For eighteen months, the 350th's

part was to stay with the vital shipping, alert for the Luftwaffe to make the first move.

But in the climactic campaign of the North Apennines, the 350th was given orders to carry the fight to the enemy. Between 23 December 1944 and 28 April 1945, the 350th immobilized 171 enemy aircraft. Of these, 91 were destroyed on the ground and 17 in the air, 56 were damaged on the ground and 8 damaged in the air. 97 fuel storage points were set ablaze.

This destruction ended the life of the Luftwaffe.

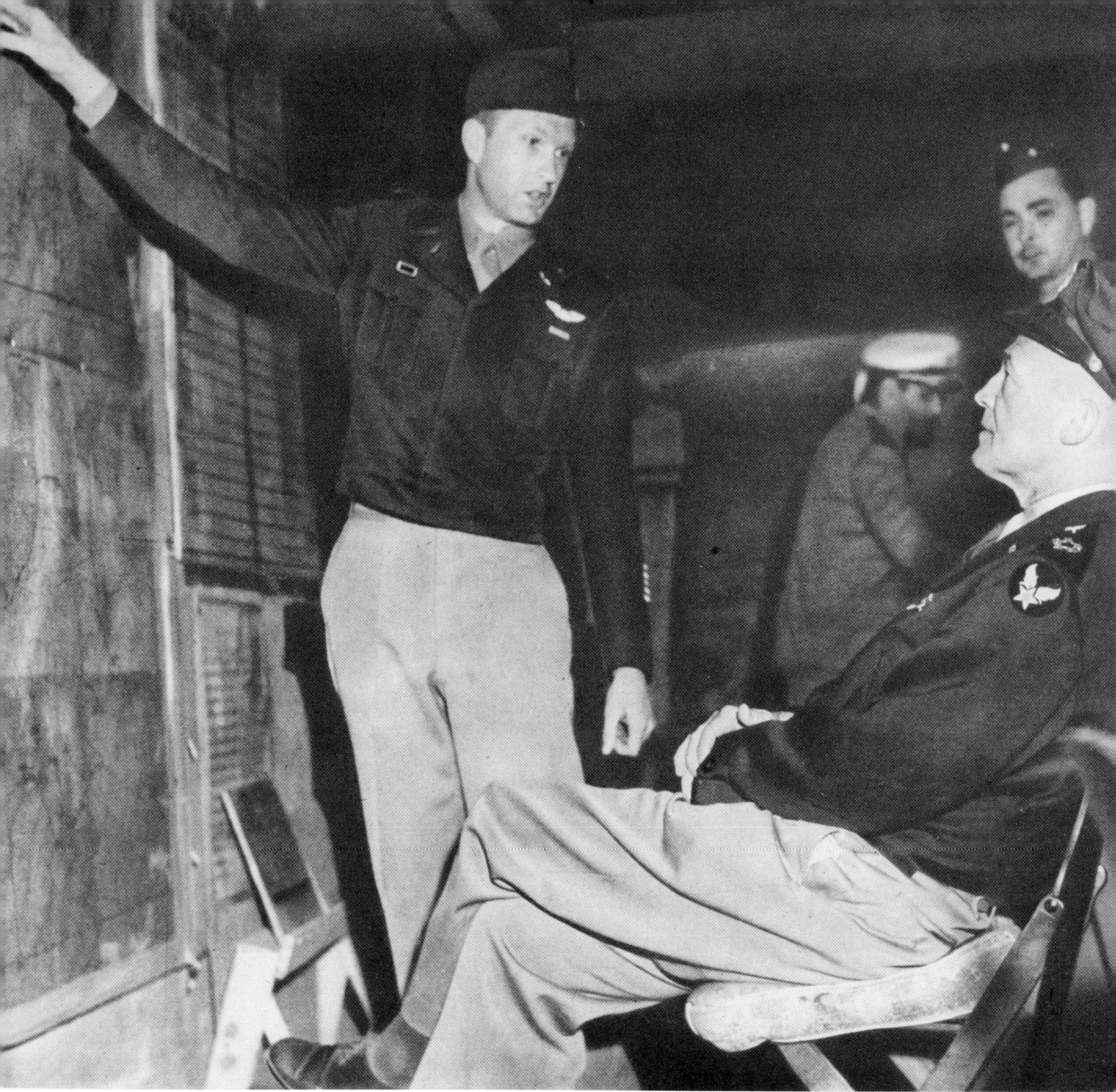

## General of the Army H. H. Arnold Reviews 350th Operations

Colonel Ariel W. Nielsen, Commander of the 350th Fighter Group throughout five campaigns describes the work in the Battle for the Apennines. Brigadier General Robert S. Israel Jr., Commanding General of XXII Tactical Air Command, accompanies General Arnold on his inspection.

# *FOREWORD*

Three Squadrons made the 350th Fighter Group name mean much in the record of the Mediterranean Campaign. These Squadrons - the 345th Fighter Squadron, the 346th Fighter Squadron and the 347th Fighter Squadron - are the 350th Group. Each one has its own story of distinctive fighting spirit, tactics, maintenance, ingenuity, initiative, and results.

When the separate histories of the Squadrons are published, they will tell of the accomplishments of individuals, the life of the men, the satisfactions and hardships, the bright side and the other side.

But until these histories are ready, this book of highlights will serve as a souvenir, a tribute from the Group to its Squadrons, an expression of the pride we all feel in a job well done, a means of telling the people at home where we have been and what we have done with the weapons they gave us.

Overseas experience for the enlisted personnel of the 350th began when 119 men, as an advanced echelon, left Harding Field, Baton Rouge, Louisiana, for England on 20 September 1942. They were the first of the ground crews which Major Robert L. Fisher was forming in the United States. When Major Fisher and his staff had completed their work in early January 1943, they had dispatched about 800 men trained for overseas duty.

By 1 October, Group Headquarters was set up at Duxford, England, ready to receive pilots from other Groups already in England, and the men from the United States; Major Richard P. Klocko, West Point '37, Group Commander, Captain Ariel W. Nielsen, Operations Officer, Captain Kelly W. Mitchim, 345th Squadron Commander, Captain John C. Robertson, 346th Fighter Squadron Commander, Captain James G. Thorsen, 347th Squadron Commander.

It was expected that the 350th would see its first action in the Moroccan Campaign, but the fighting there was so brief that the second 350th ground echelon, arriving at Casablanca 18 November 1942, heard only the last few shots that were fired, and the movement of headquarters and flight personnel from Great Britain to North Africa was postponed until January.

So with this change of plans, the beginning of the overseas experiences, both in England and North Africa, was a lean and humble period of barrel-rolling and marking time.

The heroic and historic flight of the P-39's from Great Britain to Port Layautey brought life, zest and unity to the Group in early January 1943. This 7-hour flight over enemy controlled waters was far beyond the published range of the Airacobra. It proved the skill and courage of our pilots. Sixty-two of the original pilots of the Group started out on this hazardous flight. Forty-nine landed safely, ten were forced down in Portugal, one in Spain and two were missing.

And when their first joy was to see mechanics actually equipped with tools, it was equal proof of the lean time in England, where even spark plugs remained without inspection for lack of wrenches to remove them.

Great is the contrast between the rugged beginning and the glorious end of the campaign. Between these extremes lies the hard work and successful effort of everyone concerned.

★　　　★　　　★　　　★　　　★　　　★　　　★

**The first overseas echelon Leaving Baton Rouge, La. 19 September 1942.**

★　　　★　　　★　　　★　　　★　　　★　　　★

# MEDITERRANEAN CAMPAIGN

NORTH

AJACCIO

ALGHERO

LA SENIA

ORLEANSVILLE

MAISON BLANCHE

REGHAIA

TAHER

TINGLEY

LE SER

OUJDA

THELEPTE

MEDITERRANEAN CAMPAIGN

PISA

PIOMBINO

TARQUINIA

TRE CANCELLO

CAPODICHINO

POMIGLIANO

FIDI AMOR

MONASTIR

350TH FIGHTER GROUP

# AT CASABLANCA, OUJDA, THELEPTE, LA SENIA, AND MAISON BLANCHE

## Close of the I Phase - Moroccan Campaign

The first of the eight campaigns for the Mediterranean was the shortest. Between 11 and 17 November, 1942, French Morocco and Algeria capitulated to our invasion forces. Fifteen hundred miles separated these forces from the British Eighth Army which had recaptured Tobruk and was on its way across the Libyan Desert. Now the Tunisian Campaign was to settle who was to be master of North Africa.

When the second over-seas echelon of the 350th arrived at Cazes Airfield, French Morocco, late in the evening of 19 November, there was no longer any fighting to do in that immediate area, instead there was hard labor to get the supplies in, clean up the harbor, set up depots and guard against further trouble.

The 350th put out 188 men on guard and MP duty at the airfield, and at Fedala and Sidi Marauff; 120 more men to unload and move gasoline from the port and 12 men for ordinance duty at the airfield and at Rabat, while the officers took over duties at the airfield or at the docks.

Separated from all the other materiel the men moved, was the 350th's own initial equipment, chiefly tools, airplane engines and parts and a few vehicles. In about 5 weeks over 140,000 pounds of property accumulated.

## Opening of II Phase - Tunisian Campaign

Major Nielsen arrived from Group Headquarters in England on 3 January, while during the same period more men and officers arrived. On 5 January, the Group moved to Oujda, and the pilots and planes began to come in from England. Lt. Colonel Klocko, Group Commander, arrived on the 16th. The 350th began operational flyng from the grass field at Oujda which was little better than a pasture.

Within a four week period came three hurry calls. Rush a detachment of planes and men to La Senia Airfield, Oran, (14 January) for intercept work and to give aerial protection to convoys at sea; rush another detachment to Thelepte Airfield, near Kassarine Pass, Tunisia, (6 February) for armed reconnaissance duty; then rush the detachment at Oran over to Maison Blanche, Algiers (11 February), to escort troop carrier aircraft from there to the Tunisian Front. The 345th answered the first and third calls, and the 346th answered the second call.

The 350th began to have victories and honors - and casualties, too. Captain Hoover and Lt. Hugh D. Dow each shot down an ME 109 at Thelepte. Then, among the four first losses was Lt. Colonel Klocko, shot down and taken prisoner, only a few days after he had distinguished himself by delivering a drop message to a « lost battalion », which saved it. And at Oujda, the mettle of our men was proved when Corporal Sam Chomko of the Medics pulled a pilot out of a burning A-20.

« You have done a great job. My sympathies are with you for the losses incurred ». This message from Colonel Williams, Commanding Officer of the XII Air Support Command was received by the 346th on 9 February 1943 and was the first of all the many combat commendations received by the 350th.

**Shanty life at Casablanca produced these makeshift luxuries for living.**

Note of thanks to the 350th Group
from George VI., King of England.

Many thanks for
Escort best of luck to
you
George R.I.

Chow in the early days in North Africa was served in the open. Mixed bully beef and dust was a regular meal. Most people were hungry, but nobody starved. The 350th had a good meal on Christmas Day, 1942, in one of the hangars at Casablanca. Native chickens were purchased and the "fixins" made by daily savings of flour and sugar. General John K. Cannon visited the party, and everyone felt better after his Christmas greeting when he said the 350th would soon get its airplanes.

Loading "40 and 8 cars" with engines that weighed a ton and wing parts larger than the cars was done by manpower and improvised hoists. These cars also served as pullmans.

First combat headquarters in the Group was the 346th's dugout at Thelepte, Tunisia. Everything was underground. Lt. Hugh Dow stands at the entrance of the dugout.

# AT LA SENIA ORLEANSVILLE AND LE SERS

## Continuing the II Phase, Tunisian Campaign (8 November 1942 - 13 May 1943)

During the dark February 1943 days of the Hun breakthrough at Kasserine Pass, General Spaatz' Northwest African Air Force was organized and soon after established air supremacy in the Mediterranean. General Order No. 1, 18 February 1943, assigned the 350th Fighter Group to coastal duty under the Northwest African Coastal Air Force.

From that date until it was transferred to tactical duty 18 months later, the 350th took aerial part in every major marine movement in the western Mediterranean area, including the movement of supplies to Tunisia, the amphibious operations

Open-air maintenance in North Africa.

at Pantelleria, Sicily, Salerno, Anzio, Corsica, Elba and Southern France, as well as the steady flow of shipping day in and day out.

In this period, the 350th defended most of the existing great capital ships of the Allied Navies and the Allied Merchant Fleets both in port and at sea. No other

Word came that the 350th was needed on the islands of Sardinia and Corsica, for three reasons: to defend the airfields in Southern Sardinia where medium bombers were to be based; to defend the naval base to be established at La Maddalena in the Straits of Bonifacio between Sardinia and Corsica; and to engage in armed reconnaissance from Corsica to the Ligurian shores of Italy.

Accordingly the 345th was sent to Alghero Airfield in Northern Sardinia, the 346th was sent to Elmas Airfield in Southern Sardinia, and the 347th to the east coast of Corsica at Ghisonaccia. These moves were staggered by echelons and squadrons, but the 350th left North Africa between October to December 1943. and its squadrons were pioneers at each of the newly captured airfields on the Mediterranean Islands.

Group headquarters took command of Alghero/Fertilla Airfield and in three months developed it as a base for some 2,000 Allied troops, liberating the former Axis prisoners held there, and exercising general police powers in Northern Sardinia. The 346th took responsibility for base operations at Elmas, in addition to its regular operational duties.

**Group Officer's Quarters - Ghisonaccia, Corsica.**

★          ★          ★          ★          ★          ★          ★

# AT CAPODICHINO, SIDI AMOR, POMIGLIANO, TRE CANCELLO, TARQUINIA, PIOMBINO, AND ROSIGNANO

## During the V Phase - Rome-Arno Campaign (22 January to 9 September 1944)

Each of the three winters of the Mediterranean Campaign have included long periods of stalemated operations between the opposing armies. After Naples was taken, Allied hopes for an early conquest of Rome were thwarted by the stubborn stand of the Hun at Cassino, by his fierce but unsuccessful effort to dislodge the Allied beachhead at Anzio, and by mountains, snow, rain and mud.

Shortly after the 350$^{th}$ had run diversionary flights to deceive the enemy while the Anzio landing took place, it was called upon to temporarily occupy two more bases in addition to Alghero, Elmas and Ghisonaccia. Assistance was needed from us in the Naples-Anzio region, and the Tunis-Bizerte area. The Group answered by dispatching the 347$^{th}$ Squadron from Corsica to Capodichino Airfield near Naples, by sending one half of the 345$^{th}$ aircraft to Corsica, and by sending a flight from the 346$^{th}$ to Sidi Amor Airfield, near Tunis. Group Headquarters moved to Ghisonaccia, Corsica.

The 350$^{th}$ had never been so extended as it was now, with detachments on two continents and two islands, simultaneously, and miles of water and land between them. Even so, it was plain to see that every outfit in the Mediterranean must do more than its share if the Hun was to be conquered. The 350$^{th}$ then volunteered for extra services suited to the Airacobra.

The 345$^{th}$ and 346$^{th}$ volunteered to do attack work against enemy radar installations on the west coast of Italy. During January and February, as an extra duty, they discovered and knocked out most of these enemy warning stations within a 150' mile radius of base, and harassed enemy communications.

The 347$^{th}$ volunteered to do armed reconnaissance to the heavily defended enemy harbors of Piombino, Leghorn, Porto Ferrajio, La Spezia, etc., and when the 347$^{th}$ went to the Naples-Anzio territory, the 345$^{th}$ Detachment took over this reconnaissance work.

While engaged in this reconnaissance, the 345$^{th}$ fitted two Airacobras to carry 500 pound bombs and demonstrated amazing accuracy in dive-bombing with the P-39 on a test flight on 7 March. This was the first time the Airacobra had been used for dive bombing in the European Theatre.

Brigadier General L. C. Craigie had succeeded Brigadier General Graves as Commanding General of the 63rd Fighter Wing, after General Graves was lost while leading a medium bomber attack. Brigadier General Craigie encouraged the 350th in its bombing plans, and soon had convinced Major General Cannon that the 350th could continue its regular duties and at the same time take part in the famous « Operation Strangle » designed to choke off the Hun's roads and railroads to the Cassino front.

The 347th returned from Italy to Corsica a week later and the other squadrons voluntarily sent as many ships as they could spare each day up to Corsica

The Group Headquarters building - Aghione, Corsica.

to exploit the Airacobra as a dive bomber. Major General Cannon assigned the 350th to interdict the coast road from Leghorn to Civitavecchia, and this objective, was accomplished with about 100 voluntary missions between 15 March and 15 April.

For its heroism at this time, especially on 6 April 1944, the 350th Fighter Group was cited in War Department General Orders. The citation appears on another page. The initial recommendation was made by Brigadier General L. C. Craigie.

« Operation Strangle » undertaken by the entire 12th Air Force, was so successful in cutting off enemy supplies, that on 13 May the Allies began a breakthrough at Cassino, and by 4 June, Rome had fallen.

With the conclusion of « Operation Strangle », Group Headquarters took on a new duty, command of Aghione Airfield, Corsica, moving there with the 347th Squadron on 20 May to relieve the crowded conditions at Ghisonaccia.

Throughout the balance of the summer and early fall, the American Fifth and British Eighth Armies battled up the Italian peninsula. Florence was occupied 12 August, Pisa by 2 September, and the Arno line was controlled by the Allies by 9 September, but the Luftwaffe held firm its bases and planes in North Italy, making the defensive work of the 350th most essential.

As the Allies took more of Italy, there was more coastal protective work to do, and by now, only the 350th had the « know-how » to do it. All of Corsica, Sardinia and the Tunis-Bizerte areas were still under 350th protection. In addition, to cover West Italy from Naples northward as the armies advanced, was the problem. The bottom of the barrel was scratched for pilots, men, planes, tools, tents, transportation, food, and airfields.

None of our line men will ever forget the second-hand P-39Q's they were forced by circumstances to put into shape to replace and augment our worn P-39N's.

It may be impossible for the reader to follow the story of the deployment of the 350th Fighter Group between May and September 1944. But the record must be set forth to show how intensely the personnel were engaged at that time.

The 347th remained in Corsica to give defense there and also to be ready to operate in Sardinia as the nucleus of the 350th's part in the Invasion of Southern France, and to aid in the invasion of Elba by French Colonial troops, (18 June 1944). The 346th moved to Pomigliano, 25 June.

Between the two moves, the 346th defended all of Sardinia and Tunis-Bizerte by splitting off an echelon which served at Alghero from 27 May to 25 June, and holding the two other echelons at Elmas and Sidi Amor. Then it regrouped at Elmas for the Italy move.

As fast as these two squadrons arrived in Italy, they deployed and sent out detachments to follow the Armies into newly acquired territory. The 345th sent a detachment to Tre Cancello Airfield in the Anzio region, 12 June. It moved the main body of the squadron to Tarquinia Airfield on the heels of the Fifth Army, main body of the squadron to Tarquinia Airfield on the heels of the Fifth Army, arriving there 19 June about a week after it was cleared of Germans. They left a detachment behind at Pomigliano to coordinate with the 346th.

When the 346th arrived, it remained at Pomigliano, but sent a detachment to Piombino Airfield, north of Tarquinia, 7 July, on the heels of the retreating Hun. The entire coast from Naples to Piombino was dotted with elements of the 350th moving northward. On 1 September the 345th stationed a detachment further north at Rosignano, south of Livorno.

These elements of the 350th in Italy came under a new chain of command, and in this way new and close friendships were made, which were to carry on until the end of the Mediterranean Campaign. Brigadier General Robert S. Israel and his staff comprising the 62nd Fighter Wing, became the next higher echelon on 1 September 1944.

**Right : Sgt Perry Bryson, All-Sardinia Champ.**

# FOR THE RECORD

Improvised equipment helped win for the 350th. Inventiveness and ingenuity were necessary in every section. This device for dropping Psychological Warfare material was one of many inventions.

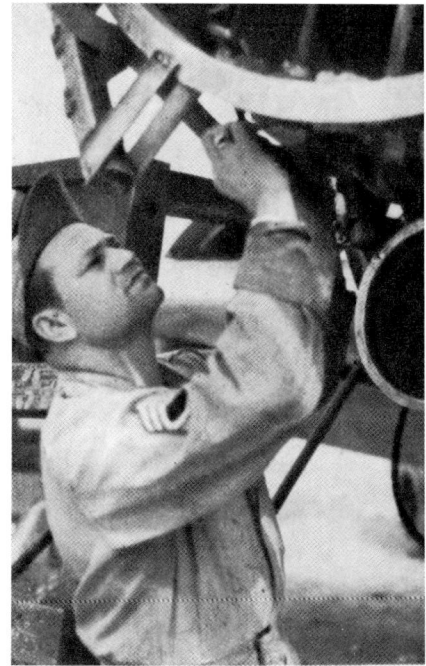

Checking the valves and oil lines. Constant inspections, and watchfulness for as near perfection as possible in mechanics, set a high record of flight and combat performance.

Inspecting the feed mechanism of the eight 50 caliber machine guns.

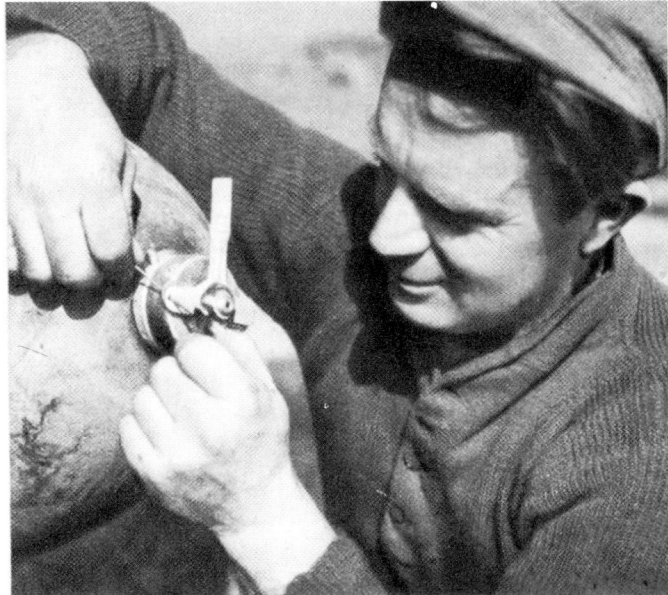

Installing the arming wire on a 500 pounder just before takeoff.

# AT BASTIA AND ALGHERO

**During the VI Phase - Southern France Invasion (15 August 1944 - 14 September 1944)**

After the long anticipated Western European Front was opened by General Eisenhower's landings in Normandy on 6 June 1944, an Allied Task Force was created in the Mediterranean to strike Southern France at the Riviera in mid-August. At Naples and Tunis, there were about 2,000 ships of all kinds ready to take off.

The 350th's part in the Southern France invasion was in the nature of a temporary extra duty, and once more proved our deftness in deployment for greatest patrol strength. Some of the task force was to pass from Naples through the Straits of Bonifacio and some would pass along the western shores of Sardinia.

Headquarters building at Alghero, Sardinia.

While waiting for this event the 347th had moved south to Ghisonaccia. Group Headquarters moved so often it was difficult to find, but after a stay at Ghisonaccia, most of the impedimenta rested at Bastia, Corsica, where communications were better.

As the invasion date approached, it seemed best to adopt Alghero, Sardinia, as a focal point from which the planes could be dispatched in all directions to cover the fleet.

The 345th and 347th temporarily put their maximum effective strength at Alghero. The 346th stayed at Naples until the bulk of the invasion fleet had left there, and then in a quick move, sent an echelon to reinforce the 350th at Alghero. Although the Luftwaffe had its bombers warmed up, and its reconnaissance caught sight of the fleet, the 350th put out so much strength again, that Jerry failed to attempt an attack. In six days, 11 to 17 August, the duty was completed, and while the 345th deployed some aircraft to Ajaccio for follow-up protection, the 350th's services were now in demand in Italy, to operate in coordination with the American Fifth Army.

Pilots being interrogated by the intelligence officer on return from a mission.

# AT TARQUINIA AND PISA

## During the VII Phase - North Apennines Campaign
## 10 September 1944 to 4 April 1945

The Wehrmacht was entrenched in the Northern Apennines. Gains against the Hun were measured in yards. This was the start of eight months during which the Italian Front was forgotten by the press, except for the casualty lists, and when people began to speculate as to whether the Allies would ever take the Po Valley. Rugged mountains, minefields, stubborn pill boxes, mud, demolition and snow held up our ground forces, and the burden of harassing the enemy and weakening his positions fell to the 12th Air Force.

By 10 September, the 350th was together at Tarquinia Airfield. All of the scattered detachments were brought in. The Group was fully equipped now with new Thunderbolts. Its pilot strength was twice what it had been in the early lean times. By 20 September it was operating in tactical coordination with the Fifth Army, under Major General Chidlaw's XXII Tactical Air Command, through the 62nd Fighter Wing, Brigadier General Robert S. Israel, Commanding. Later, Major General Chidlaw took command of the 12th Air Force, when Lt. General Cannon assumed command of the Mediterranean Allied Air Force. Brigadier General Thomas C. Darcy then commanded XXII Tactical Air Command until he was succeeded by Brigadier General Israel.

On the northwest end of Tarquinia Airfield, the 345th had its installations, and dispersal area, with Group Operations and Intelligence nearby. The 346th installations were on the south side, and the 347th to the extreme southeast. To the northwest were the bivouac areas. The 350th Thunderbolts and tents spread out as far as the eye could see, and every man of the Group was proud to look at its size and strength in one place.

The work, for both pilots and ground crews was quite different. The change-over to the big new Thunderbolts with the radial instead of inline engine, was taken in stride. These planes that required loading at least two 500 pound bombs, 3,200 rounds of ammunition, 400 gallons of gasoline and later six rockets on every mission in addition to servicing, kept everyone busy. On the average, 80 Thunderbolts of the 350th left Tarquinia every fair day, to attack vehicles and trains, roads, rails and bridges, enemy supplies of fuel and ammunition, enemy troop concentrations and enemy big guns, in the immediate battle zone or behind the enemy's lines.

The greatest difference was in the satisfaction obtained by everyone. Whereas covering the convoys had been so impersonal — and to see one convoy was to see them all — this new task gave constant variety and opportunity for individual achievement. Dozens of messages were received, such as this one from the Fifth Army: « 442 Regiment says thanks to 350th Fighter Group for a swell show. All hits on the nose. We are attacking. » or « Ground reports indicate bombing devastatingly accurate, Vergato burning. good showing ». Reports like these let squadrons of the 350th know that they were doing something worthwhile.

Three other Fighter Groups were engaged in the same campaign. Each was an old-timer in tactical work. When the records of the first ten days of operations by the four groups were published, the rookie 350th was amazed to find that it had out-fought and out-flown and out-maintained the others. It continued at the top of the list to the end of the campaign.

Certainly the 350th had learned to maintain aircraft while in coastal service where the operational requirement was so heavy. Its aggressive spirit seemed only normal. The squadrons had always put emphasis on quality; to do the most with the fewest accidents, fewest errors, most landings per tire change, and no failures while airborne. Now the words of praise began to come from all sides. The 350th earned such nick-names as « Red Hot », it flew an average of 10 % more missions because of its excellent maintenance and by flying when no one else would fly; it expended 20 % more ammunition and it brought back big scores of destruction.

The commendations, from high ranking officers of the Air and Ground Forces, were received with quiet pride, but the Group was paid one of its greatest compliments when on 7 October the First Brazilian Fighter Squadron arrived and was assigned to the operational control of the 350th. Now there were four squadrons with air strength double what the Group had in 1943, with fire power, bomb capacity, range, speed and maneuverability incomparably superior.

All in the Group who helped the Brazilians start off enjoyed doing so because the Brazilians wanted to fight the common enemy, and fight him skillfully.

Within a month they operated like veterans. They had very few replacements compared to our squadrons, and yet their courage and tirelessness was dauntless.

On 2 December, 1944, with Tarquinia a sea of mud from incessant rains, the 350th Fighter Group and First Brazilian Squadron moved 200 miles northward to Pisa San Giusto Airfield. Most of the heavy aircraft were towed to the Tarquinia runway, which was the only dry spot, to prevent their sinking in the mud. They flew out against the enemy, and returned to the new field where advance parties were waiting. There was no break in operations.

Mud and moonlight in Tarquinia.

# AT PISA

## During the VII Phase - Po Valley Campaign - 4 April to VI Day, 2 May 1945

When the ground was dry in mid-April, Allied Armies jumped off in earnest for the final blows at the Hun in Italy and the Mediterranean. Defeat for him was inevitable, the only question was how soon. The German Colonel General Von Vietinghoff surrendered to Field Marshal Sir Harold R. L. Alexander, Supreme Commander in the Mediterranean, on 2 May, 1945, in one of the swiftest phases of the entire European Campaign.

After the push was on in earnest, the 350th was visited by a newspaperman, Lt. Bill Buntin. His account of how the Thunderbolts helped is an excellent description of a combat day with the Group.

« WITH THE ITALY-BASED 12TH AIR FORCE — The push is on - and this 12th Air Force P-47 fighter-bomber outfit is « in the line », as much so as if it had marched in with pack and rifle. Smoke-blackened guns, empty bombracks, flak holes and the grimy, youthful faces of the tensely-keyed pilots - these things tell the story.

« Fourteen hours a day the Thunderbolts are over the lines bombing, strafing, slamming rockets into German strongpoints, spreading flame over German bivouac areas, searching out individual guns or oxcarts or motorcyclists, and pounding them relentlessly. All day the shuttle goes on, a new flight taking off approximately every fifteen minutes; completed flights buzzing the tower and peeling off to land; ground crews working night and day to supply gas and oil, bombs, rockets and bullets. Maintenance is continuous. It has to be.

« To a casual observer walking into the briefing room of this 12th Air Force Thunderbolt unit, it would seem that a group of young men, attired in coveralls and wearing belts from which swing .45 automatics and hunting knives, had nothing better to do than dawdle away the morning slumped in chairs, reading magazines and listening to the radio. Of the twelve or more in the room he would probably notice four standing idly by a wall map while an Intelligence Officer spoke to them in a low voice. He might notice that the radio played a popular song and that it was poorly tuned-in and that no one seemed to notice or to care. He could not miss seeing that one pilot slept stretched out on a couch, while another knelt quietly at his feet, completely absorbed in administering a hot-foot, as if it were the most important thing in the world. The others paid no attention. Also, he might have stepped upon a small, shaggy, black and white dog asleep on the floor.

« Later, the intelligence report on the mission read, as follows:

« ' Building south of town housing 105-mm gun given as target. Four aircraft bombed and destroyed house. 2$^{nd}$ gun position in building north of town rocketed and destroyed by fire. Area straffed and two additional buildings adjacent to gun position left in flames '.

« This continuous and terrific pounding, this mass onslaught from the skies is not being sustained without loss to the brave, young airmen who nurse their heavy fighters, slung with rockets, bombs and eight machine guns, down a runway and in to the flak-dizzy air over the front lines.

« This morning the weather was good at the front, but here at base the sky was overcast. Still they flew. There were appointments with the Germans which they had told the ground forces they would keep. All day they thundered down the runway and disappeared in the messy clouds hanging low overhead. By the end of the day, four had failed to return. Two collided in the overcast and crashed into a mountain. One caught fire close to the ground and plowed-in near Bologna. The other had his plane badly shot up and was forced to bail out behind the enemy lines. In war, these things are expected. One talks very little about them. What they do talk about is the « close shaves », of which there are many right now.

« Late yesterday afternoon operations were in turmoil. A flight had just returned from an armed recce (reconnaissance) mission and reported seven American tanks in the southern outskirts of Casalechio, five miles southwest of Bologna and some distance ahead of the latest bomb-release line.

« The leader of the flight, explained it to the Colonel:

« 'We were headed north on highway 64, flying low and fast, hoping to catch some Jerries on the road. Just south of Casalechio we passed over seven tanks. We were on them so suddenly that we didn't have time to identify them. Swinging with the road, we followed it a couple of miles and saw some Jerry self-propelled guns coming out of some woods. I decided to go back and look at the tanks first. We turned and were headed in when they signaled that they were ours. Sure enough, they were headed north and had the proper markings. So I said to the boys on the R/T, « Let's help them out with those babies up the road ». There were two self-propelled guns, or tanks, I don't know which, two towed bofors guns and what looked like a Jerry jeep. We went down and fed them our rockets the first round and then we came back to dust them off. After the second pass all the vehicles were burning. The Jerries had disappeared, so we sprayed the woods on either side for good measure. Then we went back and circled the tanks for nearly half an hour, hoping to give them another boost. But no more Krauts showed up, and we came home.

« Today our tankmen, braving minefield and artillery, are loud in their applause of the Thunderbolt pilots, who are leaving their approaches to the enemy littered with the burnt-out remnants of a large share of their potential opposition.

« The present Allied advance in Italy is a table supported on legs which stem out of near-to-the-front fighter-bomber bases. This table is moving, like an elevator pushed from below, up and out of the Italian boot — moving against an entrenched enemy whose divisions outnumber our own — moving because Allied airmen have achieved the defeat of the Luftwaffe in the air and are now able to concentrate their undivided attention upon the destruction of the enemy on the ground ».

**Turkeys from home at Thanksgiving and Christmas.**

The Nettuno Hotel, on the Arno River, billet for all Squadron officers in Pisa. Headquarters and Enlisted Men's billets for the 346th and 347th Squadrons and Headquarters of the 345th Squadron in Pisa.

*... « bigger bursts and blacker too,*
*88's the flak for you! »*

In the North Appenines and Po Valley campaigns, the Hun faced the flights of the 350th with over 4,000 gun positions strategically placed throughout the battle area, and not counting his hundreds of mobile weapons. At least three quarters of our flights were fired upon, intensely.

The result was a match of skill between the enemy's concentrated gun fire and the cool determination of our pilots to reach the target by deception and evasion. In the fierce fighting in the last thirty days, eight out of every two hundred aircraft flying into the battle area were damaged.

The aircraft shown above, with a huge hole in the leading edge of the wing at the gun mount, which also destroyed the vital air speed indicator, was hit near Bologna. The hole was caused by an 88 millimeter shell which passed through the wing without exploding, and fortunately without detonating the load of ammunition carried by the Thunderbolt.

At the time this happened, our aircraft had spotted vehicle tracks, and were hunting down the vehicles themselves.

The terrific impact flipped the aircraft down on its left side. By quick skill and almost superhuman effort with the stick and rudder, the pilot levelled the plane. To his amazement, he discovered that by exerting every ounce of his strength, he could fly it. With radio advice from his wing man, he reached base, safe but completely exhausted.

Such occurences were not rare.

Anti-aircraft guns hit the planes of the 350th, 522 times from 1 September, 1944 to the end of the campaign. Damaged aircraft came back to base 469 times. The pilots of those which did not return, often parachuted out, or made an emergency landing, becoming prisoners or hunted fugitives behind the enemy lines.

On most attacks, it was the duty of the pilots of the 350th to evade these guns so as to attack chosen targets. However, when flying escort to medium bombers, it was the Group's duty to go ahead of the bombers, face these guns and silence them, in order that the bombers could proceed with precision bombardment.

Another serious hazard to our aircraft came about when enemy ammunition supplies were attacked. Successful attacks frequently resulted in such a violent explosion and so much flying debris, that our planes could not escape without damage from their own havoc.

★ ★ ★ ★ ★ ★ ★

**OTHER FLAK DAMAGED AIRCRAFT**

It took skill and strength to fly them home - and plenty of help from your wingman to "talk you in".

# FORMER COMMANDERS
# OF THE GROUP

★　★　★　★　★　★　★

## Lieutenant Colonel RICHARD P. KLOCKO

**Group Commander from Activation Day, 1 October 1942, until shot down and taken prisoner, 24 February 1943, Feriana, Tunisia**

## Lieutenant Colonel MARVIN L. McNICKLE

Group Commander during the Tunisian and the Sicilian Campaigns
1 March 1943 to 6 September 1943.

**MAJOR LEE C. WELLS**
1 May 1945 - continuing

**MAJOR EDWARD J. GABOR**
27 Dec. 1943 - 1 May 1945
Killed in Action, 1 May 1945, Tolmino, Italy

**MAJOR CHARLES F. HOOVER**
7 Sept. 1943 to 27 Dec. 1943

**LT. COL. ARIEL W. NIELSEN**
4 June 1943 - 7 Sept. 1943

**MAJOR KELLY W. MITCHIM**
1 Oct. 1942 - 4 June 1943

**MAJOR CHARLES E. GILBERT, II**
27 March 1945 - continuing

# Commanding Officers of the 346 Fighter Squadron
(the Checker Board Squadron)

## Lieutenant Colonel JOHN C. ROBERTSON

**Interim Group Commander, 22 October 1944 to 5 February 1945.**
**Deputy Commander from 26 September 1943 to date.**

Commanding Officers of the 345 Fighter Squadron
(the Devil Hawk Squadron)

LT. COL. ANDREW R. SCHINDLER
10 Aug. 1944 - 25 March 1945
Missing in Action, 25 March 1945, Padova, Italy

MAJOR RALPH E. KEYES
9 April 1944 - 10 August 1944

CAPTAIN CHARNLEY K. ATWATER
3 March 1944 - 19 March 1944
Killed, 19 March 1944, Cagliari, Sardinia

CAPTAIN JOHN A. URBAN
27 Dec. 1943 - 3 March 1944
20 March 1944 - 9 April 1944

MAJOR ROBERT L. ENGLISH
26 Sept. 1943 - 27 Dec. 1943

MAJOR JOHN C. ROBERTSON
1 Oct. 1942 - 26 Sept. 1943

**MAJOR HUGH D. DOW**
26 Sept. 1944 - 22 Jan. 1945
Prisoner of war 22 Jan. 1945
18 May 1945 - Continuing

# Commanding Officers of the 347 Fighter Squadron
## (the Screaming Red Ass Squadron)

**MAJOR ALVIN H. BALLARD**
22 Jan. 1945 - 18 May 1945

**MAJOR WILBUR J. HART**
27 Aug. 1944 - 26 Sept. 1944

**MAJOR ROBERT W. RAUP**
27 May 1944 - 26 Aug. 1944 - Died of Injuries
in Action, 26 August 1944, Alghero, Sardinia

**MAJOR FRANCIS L. GRABLE**
12 Dec. 1943 - 27 May 1944

**MAJOR JAMES G. THORSEN**
1 Oct. 1942 - 12 Dec. 1943

# COMBAT PHOTOGRAPHS OF THE
## Po Valley - Alps Campaign

The following photographs were taken both during and immediately after attacks on enemy supplies, communications, and strong points during the struggle for the Po Valley. These exposures were made by cameras attached to the wings of the attacking aircraft. Some of the most spectacular results were not able to be recorded in this manner, but as a whole these give a cross section of the type of assignments carried out by the 350th Fighter Group. Attacks like these led to the strangulation of the enemy in Northern Italy.

★    ★    ★    ★    ★    ★    ★

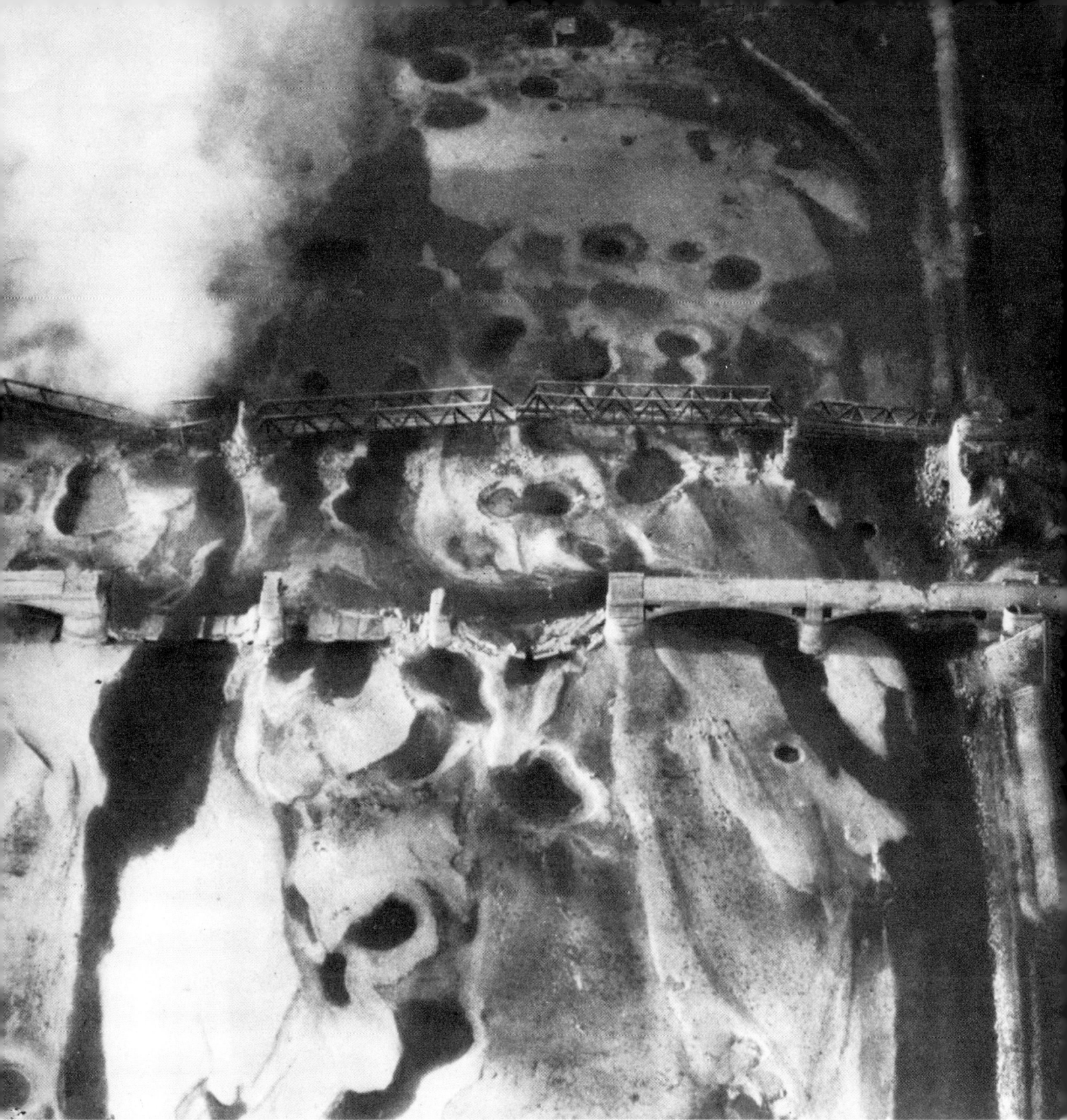

Rail and highway links severed in the important Ponte di Piave area, 8 February 1945.

German supply train goes up in smoke after bombing and strafing attack in the Po Valley on 13 March 1945.

Dive-bombers destroying a fuel dump on the outskirts of Milan, Italy, on 31 March 1945.

The strategically important Ponte di Piave rail and highway bridges lie destroyed after an attack on 10 February 1945.

Two coaches are fired by machine gun hits near Ponte di Piave on 10 February 1945.

Fuel Stores near Fontevivo, Italy, severely battered in attack launched 11 February 1945.

A well grouped cluster cut both the highway and railroad approaches to the Sassuolo bridge on 14 February 1945. A valentine to the Hun from the 350th Group.

Enemy occupied building and command posts were bracketed at the opening of the Po Valley drive on 17 February 1945.

A locomotive under straffing attack near Molzbiehl, Austria, 17 February 1945.

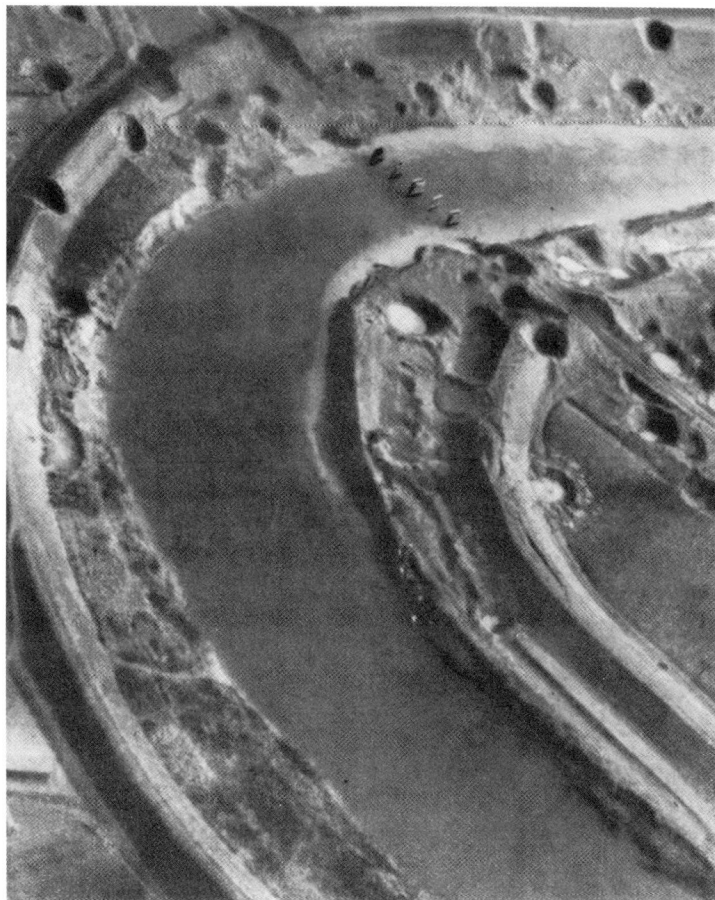

One of the vital links in the enemy's communication system interdicted at Motta di Livenza, Italy on 24 February 1945.

A closer pass by the attacking aircraft shows the above rail bridge completely destroyed.

Viaduct near Lavis, Italy knocked out on February 24, 1945.

50-caliber machine gun strikes draw smoke from freight and passenger cars in the Belluno Marshalling Yards, 12 March 1945. 2 cars at extreme right have been badly damaged by explosion.

Photo reconnaissance following dive-bombing attack on Novara Marshalling Yards, 22 March 1945, revealed at least 8 of the through lines cut. 2 coaches, 1 diesel car, 3 tank cars, 4 flats and 2 goods wagons were either hit or set on fire.

Novara, Italy, Marshalling Yards under attack on 22 March 1945.

Bombs bursting on rail viaduct at Lavis, 5 miles north of Trento, Italy, 13 March 1945.

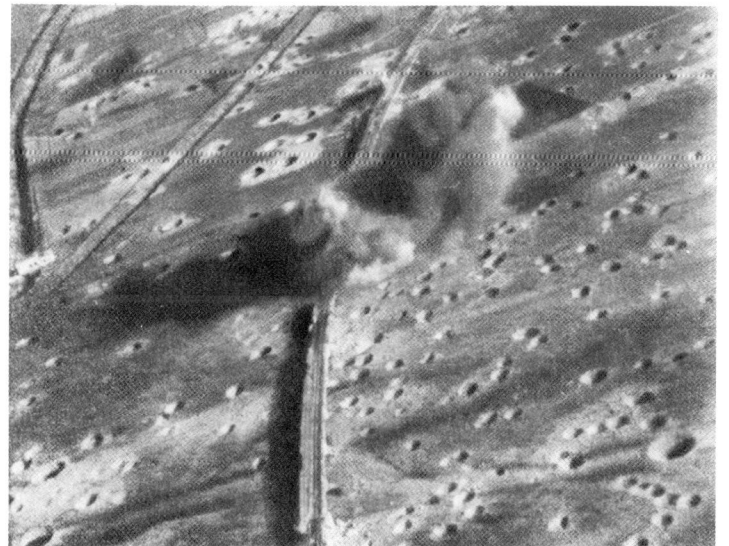

Direct hits destroy 2 spans of the high priority Lavis Viaduct on 25 March 1945.

A German Division Command Post left in flames at Calderara di Reno on 15 April 1945, during 5th Army drive northward.

Building and surrounding woods of an enemy bivouac area have been left flaming by a fire bomb attack on 16 April 1945.

A direct hit by one 500-pound demolition bomb made this clean cut of a railroad near Modena, Italy on 20 April 1945.

1000-pounders landing on runway of German-occupied Airdrome in Italy, dive-bombed on 26 February 1945.

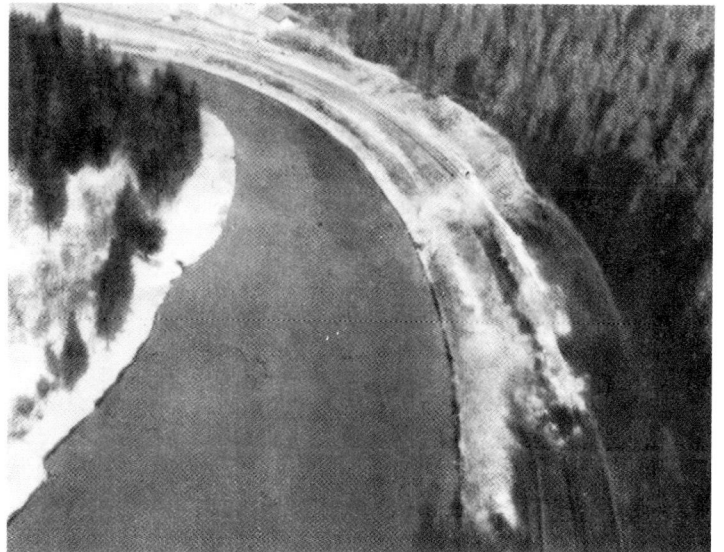

Locomotives attacked on the Brunico-Villach rail line, 27 February 1945.

Fires raging through dangerous stores of German ammunition depository near Trento, Italy on 26 February 1945, after successful bombing and straffing attack.

A great column of smoke rising from German ammunition dump near Verona, Italy, following bombing attack, 8 March 1945.

# SUMMARY OF DESTRUCTION

## In the North Apennines and the Po Valley - 1 September 1944 through 2 May 1945

### I. INTERDICTION OF ENEMY COMMUNICATIONS.

Motor Transports: 3,068 Destroyed; 2.417 Damaged.
Horse Vehicles: 1,842 Immobilized.
Rail Cars and Tankers: 1,270 Destroyed; 7,103 Damaged.
Locomotives: 339 Destroyed; 720 Damaged.
Bridges Blown: 140 Destroyed; 156 Impassable.
Rail and Highway Cuts: 1,253 Effectives.
Tunnels Blown: 33 Effectives.
Barges, Boats, Pontoons: 23 Destroyed; 266 Damaged.
Freight and Switch Yards: 165 Harassed and Damaged.
Power Stations: 6 Destroyed; 24 Damaged.
High Tension Lines: 102 Cuts.

### II. DESTRUCTION OF ENEMY SUPPLY POINTS.

Ammunition Dumps: 9 Destroyed; 121 Partly Destroyed.
Oil and Gas Dumps: 9 Destroyed; 83 Partly Destroyed.
Warehouses: 32 Destroyed; 124 Damaged.
Miscellaneous Stores Dumps: 7 Destroyed; 122 Partly Destroyed.

### III. DESTRUCTION OF SOURCES OF SUPPLY.

Refineries: 2 Destroyed; 10 Partly Destroyed.
Factories: 3 Destroyed; 160 Partly Destroyed.

### IV. DESTRUCTION OF ENEMY QUARTERS.

Barracks: 20 Destroyed; 87 Damaged.
Bivouac Areas: 5 Destroyed; 129 Partly Destroyed.
Command Headquarters: 8 Destroyed; 60 Partly Destroyed.
Occupied Towns: 10 Destroyed; 213 Partly Destroyed.

### V. DESTRUCTION OF ENEMY WEAPONS.

Armored Force Vehicles: 80 Destroyed; 119 Damaged.
Artillery Positions: 288 Destroyed; 352 Partly Destroyed.

### VI. COUNTER-AIRFORCE OPERATIONS.

Runways: 30 Crater Holes.
Hangars: 2 Destroyed; 8 Damaged.
*Aircraft in the Air: 50 Destroyed; 9 Probably Destroyed; 24 Damaged.
*Aircraft on the Ground: 108 Destroyed; 2 Probably Destroyed; 72 Damaged.
Air Warning Stations: 27 Destroyed; 68 Damaged.

* For the Entire Mediterranean Campaign.

Lieutenant General John E. Cannon awarding the Battle Honor Streamer to the 350th Group.

# BATTLE HONOR

*Extract from General Orders No. 86, War Department, Washington, D. C., 8 November 1944:*

« ...citation of the following unit... is confirmed... in the name of the President of the United States as public evidence of deserved honor and distinction. The citation reads as follows:

« The *350ᵗʰ Fighter Group* is cited for outstanding performance of duty in action against the enemy in the Mediterranean Theatre of Operations on 6 April 1944. In contributing to the success of the Operation Strangle, a vital phase of the Allied effort which resulted in the liberation of Rome, the *350ᵗʰ Fighter Group* performed above and beyond the call of duty in rendering unique and heroic services. Although assigned exclusively to air defense and reconnaissance because its battle-worn and outmoded aircraft were considered dangerously inferior to enemy fighters, this group, realizing that certain primary targets could be effectively covered only by its own airplanes, voluntarily assumed full responsibility for this coverage. Of their own volition and in addition to their designated duties, personnel within the Group converted P-39 aircraft into fighter bombers, developed suitable dive bombing tactics, and successfully interdicted supply routes at such strategic points as Tarquinia, Grosseto, Leghorn, and Pisa, while continually maintaining their regularly assigned reconnaissance patrols and sea searches covering Corsica, Sardinia, Tunisia, Italy, and the Tyrrhenian and Ligurian Seas. On 6 April 1944, the *350ᵗʰ Fighter Group*, brilliantly accomplishing a variety of commitments over this vast area, distinguished itself through outstanding courage and skill in aerial combat and in bombing and strafing ground targets. While flying 10 missions, comprising 75 sorties, on this day the group, in the face of intense antiaircraft fire, destroyed 1 highway bridge and 2 railroad bridges, 2 air warning installations, 1 barracks building and 2 trucks, and inflicted many casualties on enemy personnel and heavy damage on numerous other military buildings and vehicles. Just as one flight of six P-39 dive bombers was completing an attack on enemy communications in the Grosseto-Pisa area, they were intercepted by 10 or more ME-109's and FW-190's. Gallantly ignoring the odds against them, and despite damage to their own aircraft, the P-39 pilots unhesitatingly turned into the larger hostile formation and attacked with such skill and determination that five enemy fighters were shot down, two were damaged and the remainder driven from the battle area. Elsewhere on the same day, elements of the *350ᵗʰ Fighter Group* maintained vigilant fighter protection throughout their assigned areas, vigorously turning back enemy attacks upon Allied installations along the Eastern Coasts of Corsica and Sardinia, and on the harbor of Tunis, while other patrols conducted searches over the Mediterranean waters for enemy vessels and Allied craft in distress. The outstanding leadership, tireless devotion to duty and extraordinary heroism displayed by the officers and men of the *350ᵗʰ Fighter Group* during combat operations on 6 April 1944 have set this Group above and apart from other units involved in comparable effort during the same period and have reflected great credit upon themselves and the military service of the United States ».

# AWARD OF THE LEGION OF MERIT

JOHN H. DEJARNETTE,  Master Sergeant
ARIEL W. NIELSEN,  Colonel
JOHN C. ROBERTSON,  Lt. Colonel
GEORGE M. WIXEN,  Master Sergeant
RICHARD D. STROHL,  Master Sergeant

# AWARD OF THE SILVER STAR

* MAURICE L. ASBURY,  2nd Lieutenant
RUSSELL E. CROCKER,  Captain
JAMES D. DAILEY, JR.,  Captain (and cluster)
* JOHN DIFFENDAL,  1st Lieutenant
* MARTIN S. DOMIN,  1st Lieutenant
HUGH D. DOW,  Major
** DONALD A. ELLIS,  1st Lieutenant
FIRMAN H. FRUIT,  Captain
CHARLES E. GILBERT,  Major
MIHIEL GILORMINI,  Captain
SIGMUND E. HAUSNER,  1st Lieutenant
FRANK HECKENKAMP,  Captain
HYRUM M. KERSHAW,  1st Lieutenant
EDWIN L. KING,  Captain
** RICHARD P. KLOCKO,  Lt. Colonel
EARL D. MILLER,  Captain
FORREST W. McCARGO,  1st Lieutenant
JACK L. OGILVIE,  Captain
* GLENN R. PARISH,  1st Lieutenant
** ROBERT G. THOMPSON,  2nd Lieutenant
ROBERT C. TOMLINSON,  Captain
LEE C. WELLS,  Major

# AWARD OF THE SOLDIER'S MEDAL

ARTHUR V. AKIN, JR.,  Sergeant
EGON ANDERSON,  Master Sergeant
HAROLD J. ANDRES,  Staff Sergeant
RICHARD G. BATES,  Staff Sergeant
SAM CHOMKO,  Corporal
ROBERT E. ERWIN,  Technical Sergeant
MAJOR GORSKI,  Technical Sergeant
ALEX JACK,  Sergeant
ARCHIE O. McINTOSH,  Sergeant

# CROIX DE GUERRE WITH GOLD STAR (FRANCE)

HUGH D. DOW,  Major
EDWARD J. GABOR,  Major
FRANCIS L. GRABLE,  Major
ROBERT W. Raup,  Major

# DISTINGUISHED FLYING CROSS (GREAT BRITAIN)

MARVIN L. McNICKLE,  Colonel

# SOUTHERN CROSS (BRAZIL)

JOHN C. ROBERTSON,  Lieutenant Colonel

* Posthumous Award — ** Missing in Action when cited

# AWARD OF THE DISTINGUISHED FLYING CROSS

| | | | | |
|---|---|---|---|---|
| SHUFORD M. ALEXANDER, | 1st Lieutenant | | JACK D. ELLIOT, | Captain (and cluster) |
| SAMUEL V. ALLEN, JR., | 1st Lieutenant | | DONALD A. ELLIS, | 1st Lieutenant |
| DEAN O. ARBOGAST, | 1st Lieutenant | | ROGER C. ELLIS JR., | 1st Lieutenant |
| * MAURICE L. ASBURY, | 1st Lieutenant | | ERNEST D. FAHLBERG, | 1st Lieutenant |
| HAROLD E. BABB, | Captain | | * GENE M. FISHER, | 1st Lieutenant |
| ** ADDISON A. BACHMAN, | 1st Lieutenant | | BERNELL A. FORSTER, | 1st Lieutenant |
| RONALD O. BADE, | 1st Lieutenant | | ALVIN R. FRANEK, | 1st Lieutenant |
| ALVIN H. BALLARD, | Major | | FIRMAN H. FRUIT, | Captain |
| ** DEMPSEY E. BALLARD, | Captain | | EDWARD J. GABOR, | Major (and cluster) |
| HOWARD L. BARTON, | 1st Lieutenant | | CHARLES E. GILBERT, II, | Major (and cluster) |
| DWIGHT S. BECKHAM, | Captain | | MIHIEL GILORMINI, | Captain |
| ELMER L. BELCHER, | Captain (and cluster) | | FRANCIS L. GRABLE, | Major |
| JOHN E. BERGERON, | 1st Lieutenant | | DALE E. HANN, | Captain |
| CLAYTON P. BLAKE, | Captain | | * WILLIAM E. HARDIN, | 1st Lieutenant |
| HORACE W. BLAKENEY, | Captain | | ROBERT K. HARTLEY, | Captain |
| ROY E. BOETTCHER, | Captain | | SIGMUND E. HAUSNER, | 1st Lieutenant |
| DON B. BRAMLEY, | 2nd Lieutenant | | FRANK HECKENKAMP, | Captain |
| DARWIN G. BROOKS, | Captain | | WILLIAM E. HOSEY, | 2nd Lieutenant |
| DON E. BRYSON, | Captain | | CHARLES F. HOOVER, | Major |
| BENJAMIN B. BUEHLER, JR., | 1st Lieutenant | | DONALD J. IGOU, | 1st Lieutenant |
| MARIUS A. BUGNAND, JR., | Captain | | JOHN F. JAMES, | 1st Lieutenant |
| CHARLES H. BURGESS, | Captain | | HYRUM W. KERSHAW, | 1st Lieutenant |
| ** ROBERT E. BUSER, | 1st Lieutenant | | BERTELL W. KING, JR., | Captain |
| * EARL CALHOUN, | 2nd Lieutenant | | EDWIN L. KING, | Captain |
| JOE H. CANION, | 1st Lieutenant | | LEWIS J. KLASS, | Captain |
| WILLIAM M. CAREY, JR., | 1st Lieutenant | | RAYMOND L. KNIGHT, | 1st Lieutenant |
| * ZANE E. CARLSON, | Captain | | ALFRED A. KOWALSKI, | 2nd Lieutenant |
| ROGER E. CLEMENT, | 1st Lieutenant | | EDWIN R. KREGLOH, | Captain |
| * KENNETH E. CLIFTON, | 1st Lieutenant | | CHARLES W. LAMBERT, | 1st Lieutenant |
| LEECROY CLIFTON, | 1st Lieutenant | | JAMES K. LEVY, | 1st Lieutenant |
| RUSSELL E. CROCKER, | Captain | | MARLAND O. MARSHALL, | Captain |
| THOMAS L. CRULL, | 1st Lieutenant | | WILLIAM S. MARSHALL, | 1st Lieutenant |
| HAROLD C. CUNNINGHAM, | 1st Lieutenant | | ** LLOYD F. MARTIN, | 2nd Lieutenant |
| JAMES D. DAILEY, JR., | Captain | | RAYMOND L. MATHEWS, | 1st Lieutenant |
| ROBERT S. DAVIS, | Captain | | ALBERT M. MATTHEWS, | 1st Lieutenant |
| JAMES J. DELVIN, | Captain | | IIUGII E. McCALL, | Captain |
| JOE W. DICKERSON, | Captain | | LEE J. MERKEL, | Captain |
| MAX C. DIDERICH, | 1st Lieutenant | | FREDERICK H. MICHEL, | Major (and 2 clusters) |
| ROBERT E. DOLAN, | 1st Lieutenant | | GEORGE W. MILES, | Major |
| HUGH D. DOW, | Major | | EARL D. MILLER, | Captain |
| CHARLES C. EDDY, JR. | 1st Lieutenant | | * WALTER R. MILLER, | F/O |

| | | | |
|---|---|---|---|
| WENDELL D. MILLER, | 1st Lieutenant | MICHAEL W. SHARECK, JR., | Captain |
| RONALD R. MILLS, | 1st Lieutenant | WILLIAM SIEVERT, JR., | 1st Lieutenant |
| ROBERT K. MORROW, | Captain | FREDERICK N. SMITH, JR., | Captain |
| LORN K. NICHOLS, | 1st Lieutenant | HARVEY C. SMITH, | Captain (and cluster) |
| ARIEL W. NIELSEN, | Colonel | ALEXANDER W. STEWART, | Captain |
| WILFRED E. NOVOTNY | 1st Lieutenant | HOMER J. ST. ONGE, | 1st Lieutenant |
| JESSE C. O' BRIEN, | Captain | RICHARD P. SULZBACH, | |
| JACK L. OGILVIE, | Captain | | 1st Lieutenant (and cluster) |
| EDWARD M. OLSON, | 2nd Lieutenant | HENRY E. TATUM, | 1st Lieutenant |
| WILLIAM H. PAGE, | Major | ROBERT B. TAYLOR, | 2nd Lieutenant |
| PHILIP L. PEOPLES, | 1st Lieutenant | CHARLES R. THOMAS, JR., | Captain |
| JOHN W. PHELAN | 1st Lieutenant | JAMES THOMAS, | 1st Lieutenant |
| JOSEPH F. PICKEREL, | 1st Lieutenant | KENNETH W. THOMASON, | Captain |
| PAUL A. PLOTT, | 1st Lieutenant | ALBERT B. THOMPSON, JR., | 1st Lieutenant |
| JOHN E. POWERS, | 2nd Lieutenant | ROBERT V. THORNBLAD, | Captain |
| COLUMBUS E. PRICE, | 1st Lieutenant | CHARLES E. THORNBURGH | 1st Lieutenant |
| JOHN F. PRINCE, | 1st Lieutenant | JAMES G. THORSEN, | Major |
| DOYCE G. PYE, | 1st Lieutenant | ROBERT C. TOMLINSON | Captain |
| ROBERT W. RAUP, | Major (and cluster) | SAMUEL J. TRAVE, JR., | 1st Lieutenant |
| JACK H. REAMS, | 1st Lieutenant | GILBERT VIZCARRA, | 1st Lieutenant |
| BOBBY J. RHAY, | 1st Lieutenant | WILLIAM H. WAECHTER, | 2nd Lieutenant |
| PHILLIP M. RICE, | 1st Lieutenant | HENRY C. WALLACH, | Captain |
| JOHN C. ROBERTSON, | Lt. Colonel | JOHN S. WATERMANN, III, | Captain |
| WILLIAM T. ROGERS, | 1st Lieutenant | ARTHUR WEIDA, | 1st Lieutenant |
| VIRGIL B. ROUSH, | 1st Lieutenant | LEE C. WELLS, | Major |
| PAUL B. RUDISILL, | 1st Lieutenant | JOHN R. WENZEL, | 1st Lieutenant |
| ANDREW R. SCHINDLER, | | CHARLES F. WHEATON, | 1st Lieutenant |
| | Lt. Colonel (and cluster) | CLIFF M. WHITEHEAD, | 1st Lieutenant |
| ARTHUR F. SCHRAMM, | Captain | JAMES H. YOUNG, | 1st Lieutenant |
| GROVER H. SHANNON, | 1st Lieutenant | RICHARD C. YOUNG, | Captain |

★　　　★　　　★　　　★　　　★　　　★　　　★

# AWARD OF THE AIR MEDAL

CONRAD D. ABBITT, 1st Lieutenant, 2 clusters
EDWARD M. ADAMS, 1st Lieutenant, 4 clusters
SHUFORD M. ALEXANDER, JR.,
     1st Lieutenant, 2 clusters
JULIUS M. ALLEMAND,
     2nd Lieutenant, 1 cluster
SAMUEL V. ALLEN, JR.,
     1st Lieutenant, 2 clusters
ROBERT E. ANDERSON,   2nd Lieutenant
WAYNE P. ANDERSON,   2nd Lieutenant
DEAN O. ARBOGAST, 1st Lieutenant, 4 clusters
STEPHEN D. ARMSTRONG, Captain, 4 clusters
MAURICE L. ASBURY, 1st Lieutenant, 4 clusters
JULIAN B. ASHLEY, F/O,   1 cluster
EDWARD M. AYRES,   Major, 4 clusters
HAROLD E. BABB,   Captain, 5 clusters
ADDISON A. BACHMAN,
     1st Lieutenant, 4 clusters
RONALD O. BADE,  1st Lieutenant, 5 clusters
GRANT W. BAGLEY, 1st Lieutenant, 4 clusters
ELDON C. BALDWIN,   1st Lieutenant
ALVIN H. BALLARD,   Major, 4 clusters
DEMPSEY E. BALLARD,  Captain, 4 clusters
WESLEY T. BALLARD,   1st Lieutenant
HAROLD E. BANGERTER,  Captain, 5 clusters
PHILIP S. BARBER,  2nd Lieutenant, 1 cluster
GALEN T. BARNES,  1st Lieutenant, 4 clusters
HOWARD L. BARTON, 1st Lieutenant, 5 clusters
ARMANDO BAUMANN, 1st Lieutenant, 4 clusters
JAMES M. BECK, JR.,  2nd Liutenant, 1 cluster
DWIGHT S. BECKHAM,  Captain, 5 clusters
IVAN L. BEHEL,   Captain, 2 clusters
ELMER L. BELCHER,  Captain, 7 clusters
BONHAM F. BLACKBURN, JR.,
     1st Lieutenant, 4 clusters
CLAYTON P. BLAKE,  Captain, 4 clusters
HORACE W. BLAKENEY, Captain, 6 clusters
ROY E. BOETTCHER,  Captain, 5 clusters
GEORGE W. BOLLINGER, Captain, 5 clusters
DON B. BRAMLEY,  2nd Lieutenant, 1 cluster
RODNEY I. BRANDSTROM,
     2nd Lieutenant, 4 clusters
CARL L. BRAZIL,  2nd Lieutenant, 1 cluster
DARWIN G. BROOKS,  Captain, 5 clusters
RICHARD J. BROWN, JR.,
     2nd Lieutenant, 4 clusters
DON E. BRYSON,   Captain, 4 clusters
BENJAMIN B. BUEHLER, JR.,
     1st Lieutenant, 3 clusters

MARIUS A. BUGNAND, JR., Captain, 7 clusters
** ROBERT E. BUSER,  2nd Lieutenant, 1 cluster
CHARLES H. BURGESS,  Captain, 5 clusters
JOHN W. BUYERS,     Major
CHARLES BYRKET,   1st Lieutenant
JOHN B. BYRN,  2nd Lieutenant, 1 cluster
THOMAS W. BYRNES, 1st Licutenant, 2 clusters
* EARL CALHOUN,  2nd Lieutenant, 1 cluster
FRANK W. CAMPBELL, 1st Lieutenant, 1 cluster
JOE H. CANION,  1st Lieutenant, 4 clusters
WILLIAM M. CAREY, JR.,
     1st Lieutenant, 3 clusters
ZANE E. CARSON,   Captain, 4 clusters
HARRY R. CARNEY, 1st Lieutenant, 3 clusters
ROBERT L. CLARK,  1st Lieutenant, 2 clusters
* ROBERT H. CLAYTON,
     2nd Lieutenant, 1 cluster
ROGER E. CLEMENT, 1st Lieutenant, 3 clusters
* KENNETH E. CLIFTON,
     1st Lieutenant, 3 clusters
LEECROY CLIFTON, 1st Lieutenant, 2 clusters
JACK M. COLLINGSWORTH,  1st Lieutenant
RUPERT P. COLLINS, 1st Lieutenant, 5 clusters
ROSS T. COMBEST,  1st Lieutenant, 2 clusters
WILLIAM N. COOMBS, 1st Lieutenant, 3 clusters
JOHN P. CORDOVA, 1st Lieutenant, 2 clusters
ROBERT J. COYLE,   1st Lieutenant
RUSSELL E. CROCKER,  Captain, 7 clusters
THOMAS L. CRULL, 1st Lieutenant, 4 clusters
HAROLD C. CUNNINGHAM,
     1st Lieutenant, 3 clusters
JAMES D. DAILEY, JR.,  Captain, 4 clusters
RICHARD W. DAMBRUN,
     1st Lieutenant, 4 clusters
JOHN O. DANIELS,   Captain, 1 cluster
ROBERT S. DAVIDSON,  Captain, 2 clusters
JOHN R. DAUB, JR.,  1st Lieutenant, 3 clusters
JAMES C. DAUGHERTY,  2nd Lieutenant
ROBERT S. DAVIS,   Captain, 7 clusters
JAMES J. DELVIN,   Captain, 4 clusters
JOE W. DICKERSON,  Captain, 4 clusters
CLARENCE B. DICKINSON,  1st Lieutenant
MAX C. DIDERICH, 1st Lieutenant, 5 clusters
* JOHN E. DIEMER,   2nd Lieutenant
ROBERT A. DIETRICH,  Captain, 1 cluster
JOHN DIFFENDAL, 1st Lieutenant, 3 clusters
JAMES A. DOHERTY, 1st Lieutenant, 3 clusters
ROBERT E. DOLAN, 1st Lieutenant, 4 clusters
MARTIN S. DOMIN, 1st Lieutenant, 4 clusters

CEDRIC D. DOOLEY, Captain, 5 clusters
NICHOLAS S. DORMEY, Captain, 4 clusters
EDWARD L. DORSEY, 1st Lieutenant, 2 clusters
LOWELL E. DOUGHERTY,
                    1st Lieutenant, 4 clusters
GLENN A. DOW, 1st Lieutenant, 2 clusters
HUGH D. DOW, Major, 7 clusters
VINCENT J. DUGAN, 1st Lieutenant, 1 cluster
GORDON C. DUNCAN, 1st Lieutenant, 4 clusters
FLOYD W. EASTERWOOD, JR.,
                    2nd Lieutenant, 2 clusters
CHARLES C. EDDY, JR.,
                    1st Lieutenant, 5 clusters
JACK D. ELLIOTT, Captain, 6 clusters
JAMES V. ELLIOTT, Captain, 2 clusters
CURTIS H. ELLIS, 2nd Lieutenant, 4 clusters
DONALD A. ELLIS, 1st Lieutenant, 2 clusters
ROGER C. ELLIS, JR., 2nd Lieutenant
ROBERT L. ENGLISH, Major, 3 clusters
PETER J. FAGAN, JR., 1st Lieutenant, 4 clusters
EARNEST D. FAHLBERG,
                    1st Lieutenant, 4 clusters
GENE M. FISHER, 1st Lieutenant, 3 clusters
LESTER C. FLOYD, 1st Lieutenant, 2 clusters
BERNELL A. FORSTER, 1st Lieutenant, 3 clusters
* RUDOLPH H. FOSE, F/O
CHARLES V. FOWLES, Captain, 2 clusters
ALVIN R. FRANEK, 1st Lieutenant, 2 clusters
ANDREW W. FREEBORN,
                    1st Lieutenant, 1 cluster
FIRMAN H. FRUIT, Captain, 4 clusters
* EDWARD J. GABOR, Major, 10 clusters
EDWARD F. GALLUP, 1st Lieutenant, 5 clusters
CHARLES A. GARRETT,
                    1st Lieutenant, 3 clusters
CHARLES E. GILBERT, II, Major, 8 clusters
PHILIP R. GILBERT, 2nd Lieutenant
MIHIEL GILORMINI, Captain, 4 clusters
MELVIN M. GOIN, Captain, 3 clusters
THOMAS E. GOMEZ, 2nd Lieutenant
** NORBERT J GORSKI,
                    1st Lieutenant, 3 clusters
FRANCIS L. GRABLE, Major, 5 clusters
* RICHARD G. GREGGERSON, 2nd Lieutenant
DALE E. HANN, Captain, 4 clusters
MILTON HARBER, 2nd Lieutenant
* WILLIAM E. HARDIN, 1st Lieutenant, 1 cluster
WILBUR L. HART, Major
ROBERT K. HARTLEY, Captain, 4 clusters
SIGMUND E. HAUSNER,
                    1st Lieutenant, 3 clusters
HOWLAND HAYES, 2nd Lieutenant

WILLIAM P. HAZLEGROVE, JR., 2nd Lieutenant
FRANK HECKENKAMP, Captain, 4 clusters
JAMES H. HENDON, 1st Lieutenant, 3 clusters
ALVA D. HENEHAN, 1st Lieutenant, 4 clusters
ARVILLE J. HENSLEY, 1st Lieutenant, 4 clusters
CHARLES W. HICKMAN,
                    1st Lieutenant, 3 clusters
DUANE D. HITCHCOCK,
                    1st Lieutenant, 3 clusters
EARL A. HOAG, 1st Lieutenant, 3 clusters
RICHARD P. HOLMES, 1st Lieutenant, 2 clusters
CHARLES F. HOOVER, Major, 4 clusters
WILLIAM E. HOSEY, 2nd Lieutenant, 3 clusters
NORMAN K. HUBBARD
                    1st Lieutenant, 2 clusters
JAMES J. HUDSON, 1st Lieutenant, 7 clusters
RICHARD E. HUNTER, 2nd Lieutenant
DONALD J. IGOU, 1st Lieutenant, 3 clusters
RAY ILICH, 1st Lieutenant, 4 clusters
WILLIAM B. JACKSON, Captain, 3 clusters
INGVAR JACOBSEN, 1st Lieutenant, 3 clusters
JOHN F. JAMES, 1st Lieutenant, 4 clusters
GEORGE B. JAMESON, Captain, 4 clusters
CHESTER C. JENNINGS, JR.,
                    2nd Lieutenant, 1 cluster
JOHN P. JERUE, 1st Lieutenant, 1 cluster
ROBERT G. JOHNSON, 2nd Lieutenant, 1 cluster
BENJAMIN W. JONES, 2nd Lieutenant, 1 cluster
ROY N. JUDAH, 1st Lieutenant, 4 clusters
FRANK C. JUDIA, 1st Lieutenant, 3 clusters
HAROLD A. KARR, F/O, 1 cluster
JOSEPH R. KELLIHER, Captain, 2 clusters
HYRUM W. KERSHAW, 1st Lieutenant, 4 clusters
RALPH E. KEYES, Lt. Colonel, 1 cluster
JOHN E. KIBURZ, 1st Lieutenant, 3 clusters
BERTELL W. KING, JR., Captain, 5 clusters
EDWIN L. KING, Captain, 5 clusters
RICHARD W. KIPP, 1st Lieutenant, 2 clusters
DONALD B. KIRBY, F/O
LEWIS J. KLASS, Captain, 6 clusters
RICHARD P. KLOCKO, Lt. Colonel
RAYMOND L. KNIGHT,
                    1st Lieutenant, 5 clusters
VERNON E. KOENIG, Captain, 4 clusters
RICHARD W. KOESTER,
                    1st Lieutenant, 2 clusters
RUSSEL F. KOLLAR, 1st Lieutenant, 3 clusters
ALFRED A. KOWALSKI,
                    2nd Lieutenant, 5 clusters
EDWIN R. KREGLOH, Captain, 7 clusters
CHARLES W. LAMBERT,
                    1st Lieutenant, 4 clusters
RICHARD E. LANGDON,
                    1st Lieutenant, 5 clusters

* Last citation posthumous — ** Missing in Action when cited

ANDREW J. LANGSTON, F/O
JOSEPH A. LANHEADY, JR.,
              2nd Lieutenant, 1 cluster
JAMES K. LEVY, 1st Lieutenant, 5 clusters
LOUIS G. LIND, 2nd Lieutenant, 1 cluster
GERALD B. LOWE, 1st Lieutenant, 3 clusters
HUGH L. LYNCH, 2nd Lieutenant
COMER W. LYNN, 1st Lieutenant, 2 clusters
RONALD G. MAC DONALD, 1st Lieutenant
JAMES T. MADDERRA, JR.,
              1st Lieutenant, 3 clusters
VINCENT J. MALONE, 1st Lieutenant, 3 clusters
WILLIAM H. MANKE, 1st Lieutenant, 3 clusters
MARLAND O. MARSHALL, Captain, 2 clusters
WILLIAM S. MARSHALL,
              1st Lieutenant, 4 clusters
LLOYD F. MARTIN, 2nd Lieutenant
RAYMOND L. MATHEWS,
              1st Lieutenant, 5 clusters
ALBERT W. MATTHEWS,
              1st Lieutenant, 3 clusters
SAMUEL MAYERSON, 1st Lieutenant, 2 clusters
HUGH E. McCALL, Captain, 6 clusters
FORREST W. McCARGO,
              1st Lieutenant, 2 clusters
ROYCE L. McCLESKEY, F/O
JOHN J. McFADDEN, 2nd Lieutenant
WILLIAM H. McKENZIE,
              1st Lieutenant, 1 cluster
KITT R. McMASTER, Captain, 5 clusters
LEE J. MERKEL, Captain, 3 clusters
FREDERICK H. MICHEL, Major, 8 clusters
KIMBER M. MIDDLETON,
              1st Lieutenant, 3 clusters
GEORGE W. MILES, Major, 4 clusters
EARL D. MILLER, Captain, 5 clusters
SAMUEL M. MILLER, 1 Lieutenant, 4 clusters
WALTER R. MILLER, F/O, 2 clusters
WENDELL D. MILLER, 1st Lieutenant, 4 clusters
ROBERT A. MILLS, F/O
RONALD R. MILLS, 1st Lieutenant, 7 clusters
WALTER F. MORRISON,
              2nd Lieutenant, 2 clusters
ROBERT K. MORROW, Captain, 6 clusters
LEROY J. MORSHEIMER,
              1st Lieutenant, 3 clusters
THOMAS F. MUNRO, 1st Lieutenant, 5 clusters
LEONARD L. NELSON, 1st Lieutenant, 3 clusters
GEORGE A. NEWMAN, JR., Captain, 1 cluster
LORN K. NICHOLS, 1st Lieutenant, 4 clusters
ARIEL W. NIELSEN, Colonel, 4 clusters
WILLIAM G. NISBET, 1st Lieutenant, 2 clusters
WILFORD E. NOVOTNY,
              1st Lieutenant, 2 clusters

WILLIAM V. OAKES, 1st Lieutenant, 4 clusters
JESSE C. O'BRIEN, Captain, 5 clusters
JACK L. OGILVIE, Captain, 6 clusters
RICHARD A. OLNEY, 2nd Lieutenant, 1 cluster
CLARENCE F. OLSON, 1st Lieutenant, 3 clusters
EDWARD M. OLSON, 2nd Lieutenant, 3 clusters
RICHARD P. OSBERG, 2nd Lieutenant, 3 clusters
** EDMUND P. OZIMEK, 2nd Lieutenant
WILLIAM H. PAGE, Major, 6 clusters
BURWELL S. PALMER, 1st Lieutenant, 3 clusters
* GARWIN C. PAPE, 2nd Lieutenant, 1 cluster
GLENN R. PARISH, 1st Lieutenant, 2 clusters
JOHN J. PARKER, 2nd Lieutenant, 2 clusters
ROBERT E. PASHO, 1st Lieutenant, 1 cluster
WILLIAM E. PATTERSON,
              2nd Lieutenant, 1 cluster
JOHN B. PAYSINGER, 1st Lieutenant, 1 cluster
DOUGLAS T. PECK, Captain
PHILIP L. PEOPLES, 1st Lieutenant, 4 clusters
CHARLES R. PERRYMAN,
              2nd Lieutenant, 1 cluster
JOHN W. PHELAN, 1st Lieutenant, 4 clusters
LEON G. PHILBRICK, JR.
              1st Lieutenant, 4 clusters
JOSEPH F. PICKEREL, 1st Lieutenant, 4 clusters
PAUL A. PLOTT, 1st Lieutenant, 4 clusters
RICHARD R. POETON, 1st Lieutenant, 3 clusters
ROBERT W. POINDEXTER,
              1st Lieutenant, 2 clusters
WILLIAM T. POTEET, JR.,
              2nd Lieutenant, 1 cluster
JOHN E. POWERS, 1st Lieutenant, 3 clusters
COLUMBUS E. PRICE, 1st Lieutenant, 4 clusters
JOHN F. PRINCE, 1st Lieutenant, 4 clusters
ROBERT F. PURSELL, 1st Lieutenant, 4 clusters
DOYCE G. PYE, 1st Lieutenant, 3 clusters
DEBART QUARLES, JR.,
              1st Lieutenant, 4 clusters
HILTON B. RAMSEY, 1st Lieutenant, 3 clusters
ROBERT W. RAUP, Major, 4 clusters
JACK H. REAMS, 1st Lieutenant, 4 clusters
ORVIL Y. REECE, Captain, 1 cluster
ROBBY J. RHAY, 1st Lieutenant, 2 clusters
PHILLIP M. RICE, 1st Lieutenant, 2 clusters
W. A. RIZA, 2nd Lieutenant, 1 cluster
CHARLES D. ROBBINS, JR.,
              Captain, 3 clusters
JOHN C. ROBERTSON, Lt. Colonel, 4 clusters
EDWARD S. ROCK, 2nd Lieutenant
WILLIAM T. ROGERS, 1st Lieutenant
VIRGIL B. ROUSH, 1st Lieutenant, 4 clusters
HENDERSON O. ROSE, 2nd Lieutenant

PAUL B. RUDISILL, 1st Lieutenant, 3 clusters
HOMER J. ST. ONGE, 1st Lieutenant, 3 clusters
JOHN B. SANDSTEAD, 1st Lieutenant, 1 cluster
GERALD E. SANFORD, 1st Lieutenant, 3 clusters
ANDREW R. SCHINDLER, Lt. Colonel, 6 clusters
ARTHUR F. SCHRAMM, Captain, 4 clusters
RICHARD F. SEEDS, 1st Lieutenant, 1 cluster
GROVER H. SHANNON, 1st Lieutenant
MICHAEL W. SHARECK, JR.,
                 1st Lieutenant, 6 clusters
JAMES A. SHAVER, 1st Lieutenant, 4 clusters
WILLIAM SIEVERT, JR.,
                 1st Lieutenant, 4 clusters
HAROLD M. SIMMONDS, 2nd Lieutenant
SAMUEL W. SIMONTON,
                 1st Lieutenant, 4 clusters
DENNIS H. SLOAN, 2nd Lieutenant
EUGENE C. SMITH, 1st Lieutenant, 4 clusters
FREDERICK N. SMITH, JR., Captain, 6 clusters
HARVEY C. SMITH, 1st Lieutenant, 4 clusters
KENNETH B. SMITH, 1st Lieutenant, 2 clusters
KIRBY E. SMITH, 1st Lieutenant, 2 clusters
WAYNE H. SMITH, 1st Lieutenant, 1 cluster
CHARLES D. SMOCK, 1st Lieutenant, 1 cluster
CHADWICK B. SNEED, 2nd Lieutenant
WILLIAM R. SOUTHCOTT,
                 1st Lieutenant, 2 clusters
DURWARD M. STAYTON, JR.,
                 2nd Lieutenant, 1 cluster
MARK R. STEPHENS, Captain, 3 clusters
ALEXANDER W. STEWART, Captain, 4 clusters
* JAMES A. STEWART, 2nd Lieutenant, 1 cluster
GLIFFORD L. STOCKWELL,
                 1st Lieutenant, 3 clusters
ROBERT L. STRINGER, 2nd Lieutenant
ROBERT E. STUART, Captain, 4 clusters
WORDLAW R. STUART,
                 2nd Lieutenant, 2 clusters
WALTER R. STUCKER, 2nd Lieutenant, 2 clusters
RICHARD P. SULZBACH,
                 1st Lieutenant, 6 clusters
HOWARD L. SUMNER, 1st Lieutenant, 6 clusters
** WILLIAM W. SUMNER,
                 2nd Lieutenant, 2 clusters
GUY F. SWAN, JR., F/O, 1 cluster
HENRY E. TATUM, 1st Lieutenant, 4 clusters
ROBERT B. TAYLOR, 2nd Lieutenant, 1 cluster
EDGAR A. THARPE, JR., Captain, 2 clusters
EUDO E. THIBODEAU, 1st Lieutenant

CHARLES R. THOMAS, JR., Captain, 4 clusters
JAMES THOMAS, 1st Lieutenant, 4 clusters
KENNETH W. THOMASON, Captain, 6 clusters
ALBERT B. THOMPSON,
                 1st Lieutenant, 4 clusters
ROBERT G. THOMPSON,
                 2nd Lieutenant, 3 clusters
ROBERT V. THORNBLAD, Captain, 4 clusters
CHARLES E. THORNBURGH,
                 1st Lieutenant, 5 clusters
JAMES G. THORSEN, Major, 5 clusters
CHARLES W. TILBROOK,
                 1st Lieutenant, 3 clusters
ROBERT C. TOMLINSON, Captain, 8 clusters
LEON E. TRACY, 1st Lieutenant, 2 clusters
SAMUEL J. TRAVE, JR.,
                 1st Lieutenant, 3 clusters
RAY TUGGLE, 1st Lieutenant, 2 clusters
JOHN A. URBAN, Captain, 4 clusters
CARLES H. VAN REED,
                 1st Lieutenant, 4 clusters
STEPHEN J. VERME, 1st Lieutenant, 2 clusters
GILBERT VIZCARRA, 1st Lieutenant, 4 clusters
WILLIAM H. WAECHTER,
                 2nd Lieutenant, 1 cluster
SALVADOR B. WALCOTT, 2nd Lieutenant
HENRY C. WALLACH, Captain, 3 clusters
EVERETT L. WALLING,
                 2nd Lieutenant, 1 cluster
PORTER M. WASSUM, F/O, 1 cluster
JOHN S. WATERMAN, III, Captain, 2 clusters
CLINTON J. WEBBER, 2nd Lieutenant
LELAND W. WAGNER, 1st Lieutenant, 3 clusters
ARTHUR WEIDA, 1st Lieutenant, 3 clusters
LAWRENCE W. WELLS, 1st Lieutenant, 2 clusters
LEE C. WELLS, Major, 5 clusters
JOHN R. WENZEL, 1st Lieutenant, 4 clusters
CHARLES F. WHEATON,
                 1st Lieutenant, 2 clusters
CLIFF M. WHITEHEAD,
                 1st Lieutenant, 4 clusters
HAROLD J. WHITEMAN, Lt. Colonel
OSCAR M. WILKINSON, JR.,
                 1st Lieutenant, 3 clusters
NORMAN K. WILLIAMS, 2nd Lieutenant, 1 clusters
CLYDE H. WILSON, 1st Lieutenant, 2 clusters
JOHN W. WILSON, 1st Lieutenant, 1 cluster
DELBERT E. WYLDER, 1st Lieutenant, 3 clusters
JAMES H. YOUNG, 1st Lieutenant, 3 clusters
RICHARD C. YOUNG, Captain, 7 clusters

* Last citation posthumous — ** Missing in Action when cited

These listings represent the Decorations awarded during 1943, 1944, and until 9 June, 1945. Other acts and services had been recommended for consideration, but had not been awarded at the time of printing. Every effort has been made to publish this list accurately, and any errors of omission or of spelling are most unintentional and regretted. The listing is wholly unofficial.

# VICTORIES

## GROUP TOTAL

| DESTROYED: | PROBABLE: | DAMAGED: |
|---|---|---|
| In Air 50 - On Ground 108 | In Air 9 - On Ground 2 | In Air 24 - On Ground 72 |

| NAME | In air Destroyed | In air Probably Destroyed | In air Damaged | On ground Destroyed | On ground Probably Destroyed | On ground Damaged |
|---|---|---|---|---|---|---|
| ALLEN, S. V., 2nd Lt. . . . | | | | 1 | | |
| AYRES, E. M., Capt. . . . | | | | | | 2 |
| BABB, H. E., Capt. . . . . | | | | | | 3 |
| BACHMAN, A. A., 1st Lt. . | | | | | | 2 |
| BARTON, H. L., 1st Lt. . . . | 1 | | 1 | | | 1 |
| BELCHER, E. L., 1st Lt. . . | 1 | | | 2 | 1/3 | 5 |
| BERGERON, J. E., 1st Lt. | | | 1 | | | |
| BLAKENEY, H. W., 1st Lt. | 1/2 | | 1/2 | | | |
| BRANDSTROM, R. I., Lt. | 1/2 | | 1 | | | |
| BRAZIL, C. L., 2nd Lt. . . . | | | | | | 1 |
| BROOKS, D. G., 1st Lt. . . . | 1/2 | | 1/2 | 1 | | |
| BROWN, R. J., 2nd Lt. . . . | | | | 1 | | |
| BRYSON, D. E., Capt. . . . | | | | | | 3 |
| BUEHLER, B. B., 1st Lt. . . | | | | 2 | | |
| BUGNAND, M. A., Capt. . | | | | 1 | | |
| BURGESS, C. H., Captain . | 1 | | | | | |
| CLEMENT, R. E., 2nd Lt. | | | | 1 | | |
| CROCKER, R. E., Captain . | | | | 1 | | |
| DAILEY, J. D., Captain . . | 1 | 1 | 1 | 8½ | | 1½ |
| DAVIS, R. S., 1st Lt. . . . | | | | 6 | 1 | 1 |
| DOMIN, M. S., 1st Lt. . . . . | | | | 2 | | ½ |
| DOUGHERTY, L. E., Capt. | 1 | | | | | |
| DOW, H. D., Major . . . . | 2 | | 1 | 3 | 1 | |
| EASTERWOOD, F. W., F/O | | | | 1 | | |
| EDDY, C. C., 2nd Lt. . . . . | 1 | 1 | 2 | | | |
| ELLIOTT, J. D., 1st Lt. . . . | | | | 4 | | 2 |
| FAHLBERG, E. D., 1st Lt. | | | | 1 | | 1 |
| FORSTER, B. A., 1st Lt. . . | | | | 1 | | |
| FOWLES, C. V., Capt. . . . | 1 | | | | | |
| FREEBORN, A. W., 2nd Lt. | | | | 2 | | 1 |
| GABOR, E. J., Major . . . | 1/2 | | | | | |
| GARRETT, C. A., 2nd Lt. . | | | 1/2 | | | |
| GILBERT, C. E., Major . . | 2 | | | | | |
| GOMEZ, T. E., 2nd Lt. . . . | | | | 1/3 | | |
| GORSKI, N. J., 2nd Lt. . . . | | | | 1 | | |
| HANN, D. E., Captain . . | | | | | | 2 |
| HARBER, M., 2nd Lt. . . . | | | 1 | | | |
| HAUSNER, S. E., 1st Lt. . | 1 | | | 2 | | |
| HECKENKAMP, F.W., Capt. | 3 | | | | | |
| HENEHAN, A. D., 1st Lt. . | | | | 3 | | |
| HITCHCOCK, D. D., 1st Lt. | | | | 2 | | |
| HOOVER, C. F., Major . . | 1½ | | | | | |
| HOSEY, W. E., F/O . . . | 1 | | | 2 | | 2 |
| HUNTER, R. E., 2nd Lt. . . | 1 | | | | | |
| JAMES, J. F., 1st Lt. . . . | | | | | | 2 |
| JAMESON, G. B., 1st Lt. . . | 1 | | | | | |
| JONES, B. W., 2nd Lt. . . . | 1 | | | | | |
| KERSHAW, H. W., 1st Lt. | | | | 5 | | 3 |
| KING, E. L., Capt. . . . . . | | | | | | 1 |
| KLASS, L. J., Capt. . . . . . | 2 | 2 | | | | |
| KNIGHT, R. L., 1st Lt. . . . | | | | 15 | | 2 |
| KOENIG, V. E., Capt. . . . | | | 1 | | | |
| LEVY, J. K., 1st Lt. . . . . | 1 | | | | | |
| MARSHALL, M. O., Capt. . | 1 | | | | | |
| MARTIN, L. F., 1st Lt. . . . | | | | 1 | | |
| MATHEWS, R. L., 1st Lt. . | | | | | | 2 |
| McFADDEN, J. J., 2nd Lt. . | | | | 1 | | |
| McKENZIE, W. H., 2nd Lt. | 1 | | | | | |
| McMASTER, K. R., Capt. . | 3 | | | | | |
| MICHEL, F. H., Captain . | | 2 | 2 | | | 1 |
| MILLER, W. R., F/O . . . | 1 | | 1 | | | |
| MORROW, R. K., 1st Lt. . . | | | | 3 | | 2 |
| NELSON, L. L., 1st Lt. . . . | 1 | | 1 | | | |
| OGILIVIE, J. L., Capt. . . . | | | 1 | | | |
| OLSON, E. M., 1st Lt. . . . | 1 | | | | | |
| PAGE, W. H., Major . . . | | | | 3 | | 1½ |
| PARISH, G. L., Lt. . . . . . | | | | 1 | 1/3 | 2 |
| PEOPLES, P. L., Lt. . . . . | | | | | | 2 |
| PICKEREL, J. F., 1st Lt. . . | | | | 2 | | |
| PLOTT, P. A., Lt. . . . . . | | | | 1 | | |
| PYE, D. G., 1st Lt. . . . . . | | | | 1 | | |
| REAMS, J. H., 2nd Lt. . . . | | | | 1 | | |
| RHAY, B. J., 2nd Lt. . . . . | | | | 1 | | 1 |
| RICE, P. M., 2nd Lt. . . . . | | | | | | 2 |
| ROGERS, W. T., 2nd Lt. . . | | | | 1 | | |
| RUDISILL, P. B., 1st Lt. . . | 1 | | 2 | | | |
| SCHINDLER, A. R., Major | 1 | | | 1 | | |
| SHARECK, M. W., Capt. . . | | | 1 | | | |
| SMITH, K. E., 2nd Lt. . . . | 1 | | | | | |
| SMITH, W. H., 2nd Lt. . . . | | | | 1 | | |
| SQUIRES, 2nd Lt. . . . . . | | | ½ | | | |
| SULZBACH, R. P., 2nd Lt. | 3 | | | 6½ | | 1½ |
| TAYLOR, R. B., Lt. . . . . | 1 | | | | | |
| THARPE, E. A., Capt. . . . | | 1 | | | | |
| THOMASON, K. W.. . . . . | | | | 6 | | 4 |
| THOMPSON, A. B., Lt. . . . | | | | | | 1 |
| THOMPSON, R. G., Lt. . . | | | 1 | | | 1 |
| TOMLINSON, R. C., Capt.. | 2 | 1 | 1 | | | |
| TUGGLE, R., 2nd Lt. . . . . | | | | | | 1 |
| URBAN, J. A., Captain . . | 2 | | | | | |
| VAN REED, C., Captain . | 1 | | | | | |
| VERME, S. J., Lt. . . . . . | | | | | | 1 |
| WALLING, E. L., Lt. . . . . | | | | 2 | | |
| WATERMAN, J. S., Capt.. | 1 | | | | | |
| WEBBER, C. J., Lt. . . . . | | | | 1 | | |
| WELLS, L. C., Major . . . | 1 | | | | | |
| WELLS, L. W., Lt. . . . . | | | | 2 | | |
| WENZEL, J. R., Lt. . . . . | | | | 1 | | |
| WILKINSON, O. M., Lt. . | | | 1 | | | |
| WILKINSON, T., Lt. . . . . | | | | | | 2 |
| WYLDER, D. E. Lt. . . . . | 1/2 | | 2 | | | |
| YOUNG, J. H., Lt. . . . . | 1 | | | | | |
| * 350TH FIGHTER GROUP | 1 | 1 | | 2 | | 10 |

* VICTORIES CREDITED TO THE GROUP WHENEVER CORRECT CLAIMS COULD NOT BE MADE BY THE VICTORIOUS PILOTS

# HONOR ROLL

| NAME RANK | TYPE CASUALTY | DATE |
|---|---|---|
| GREENWAY, H. J., 2nd Lt. . . . . . . . . | Killed | 6 Nov. '42 |
| WEAVER, D. E., 2nd Lt . . . . . . . . . | Killed | 18 Jan. '43 |
| NELSON, H. M., 2nd Lt. . . . . . . . . | Killed in Action | 5 Feb. '43 |
| THIBODEAU, E. E., 1st Lt. . . . . . . . | Killed in Action | 17 Feb. '43 |
| SUTTON, H. W., 1st Lt. . . . . . . . . | Prisoner of War | 9 Feb. '43 |
| KLOCKO, R. P., Lt. Col. . . . . . . . . | Prisoner of War | 24 Feb. '43 |
| SCHLUTER, C. C., 2nd Lt. . . . . . . . | Killed | 24 Mar. '43 |
| DRAGOO, A. C., 2nd Lt. . . . . . . . . | Killed | 3 Apr. '43 |
| STANAGE, H. G., 2nd Lt. . . . . . . . | Killed | 3 Apr. '43 |
| TEDFORD, P. W., 1st Lt. . . . . . . . . | Killed | 6 Apr. '43 |
| HOWES, F. L., Capt. . . . . . . . . . | Killed in Action | 25 Apr. '43 |
| O'CONNOR, C. J., 1st Lt. . . . . . . . | Killed in Action | 25 Apr. '43 |
| DUGAN, V. J., 1st Lt. . . . . . . . . | Killed | 27 May '43 |
| NEWMAN, G. A., Captain . . . . . . . . | Missing in Action | 7 June '43 |
| HUNTER, R. E., 2nd Lt. . . . . . . . . | Missing in Action | 13 June '43 |
| BALLARD, W. T., 1st Lt. . . . . . . . . | Killed in Action | 6 July '43 |
| ROSE, R. D., 2nd Lt. . . . . . . . . . | Killed | 20 Aug. '43 |
| FOSE, R. H., F/O . . . . . . . . . . | Killed | 21 Aug. '43 |
| BYRN, J. B., 2nd Lt. . . . . . . . . . | Killed | 24 Aug. '43 |
| MILLS, R. A., F/O . . . . . . . . . . | Killed in Action | 16 Sept. '43 |
| JAMESON, G. B., 1st Lt. . . . . . . . . | Killed | 24 Dec. '43 |
| ALLEMAND, J. M., 2nd Lt. . . . . . . . | Killed in Action | 12 Jan. '44 |
| ANDERSON, R. E., 2nd Lt. . . . . . . . | Killed in Action | 12 Jan. '44 |
| JUDAH, R. W., 2nd Lt. . . . . . . . . | Missing in Action | 31 Jan. '44 |
| ATWATER, C. K., Capt. . . . . . . . . | Killed | 19 Mar. '44 |
| HARBER, M., 2nd Lt. . . . . . . . . . | Missing in Action | 4 Apr. 44' |
| BOYD, R. T., 2nd Lt. . . . . . . . . . | Missing in Action | 4 Apr. '44 |
| CRAVER, P. F., 2nd Lt. . . . . . . . . | Killed | 7 Apr. '44 |
| McKENZIE, W. H., 2nd Lt. . . . . . . . | Missing in Action | 9 Apr. '44 |
| LIND, L. G., 2nd Lt. . . . . . . . . . | Killed in Action | 11 Apr. '44 |
| CRAIG, T. H., 2nd Lt. . . . . . . . . . | Killed in Action | 11 Apr. '44 |
| FOWLER, F. G., 2nd Lt. . . . . . . . . | Missing in Action | 13 Apr. '44 |
| MADDERA, J. T., 1st Lt. . . . . . . . . | Prisoner of War | 20 Apr. '44 |
| POITRAS, L. W., F/O . . . . . . . . . | Killed in Action | 23 Apr. '44 |
| LEVY, J. K., 1st Lt. . . . . . . . . . | Killed in Action | 10 June '44 |
| CARPENTER, E. R., 2nd Lt. . . . . . . . | Killed in Action | 19 June '44 |
| LENT, F. L., 2nd Lt. . . . . . . . . . | Killed in Action | 26 June '44 |
| DIEMER, J. E., 2nd Lt. . . . . . . . . | Killed in Action | 12 Aug. '44 |
| RAUP, R. W., Major . . . . . . . . . | Killed in Action | 26 Aug. '44 |
| HARDIN, W. E., 2nd Lt. . . . . . . . . | Missing in Action | 5 Sept. '44 |
| CALHOUN, E., 2nd Lt. . . . . . . . . | Missing in Action | 5 Sept. '44 |
| BUSER, R. E., 1st Lt. . . . . . . . . . | Missing in Action | 16 Sept. '44 |
| CLIFTON, L., 1st Lt. . . . . . . . . . | Rescued Partisans | 22 Sept. '44 |
| McCALL, H. E., 1st Lt. . . . . . . . . | Prisoner of War | 25 Sept. '44 |
| ALEXANDER, S. M., 2nd Lt. . . . . . . . | Rescued Partisans | 1 Oct. '44 |
| SHANNON, G. H., 2nd Lt. . . . . . . . | Prisoner of War | 4 Oct. '44 |
| ELLIS, D. A., 1st Lt. . . . . . . . . . | Prisoner of War | 4 Oct. '44 |
| JERUE, J. P., 1st Lt. . . . . . . . . . | Missing in Action | 31 Oct. '44 |
| CARLSON, Z. E., Capt. . . . . . . . . | Killed in Action | 4 Nov. '44 |
| TARANTINO, P. A., 1st Lt. . . . . . . . | Killed in Action | 7 Nov. '44 |
| PAPE, G. C., 2nd Lt. . . . . . . . . . | Killed in Action | 12 Nov. '44 |
| BRAZIL, C. L., 2nd Lt. . . . . . . . . | Killed in Action | 12 Nov. '44 |
| McCARGO, F. W., 1st Lt. . . . . . . . . | Missing in Action | 9 Dec. '44 |
| REDMON, W. K., 2nd Lt. . . . . . . . . | Missing in Action | 13 Dec. '44 |
| JOHNSON, R. G., 2nd Lt. . . . . . . . | Missing in Action | 17 Dec. '44 |
| LAWSON, E. W., 2nd Lt. . . . . . . . . | Missing in Action | 17 Dec. '44 |
| MANGINO, M. L., 2nd Lt. . . . . . . . | Prisoner of War | 21 Dec. '44 |
| ANDERSON, W. P., 2nd Lt. . . . . . . . | Missing in Action | 21 Dec. '44 |
| THOMPSON, T. H., 2nd Lt. . . . . . . . | Missing in Action | 21 Dec. '44 |
| DIFFENDAL, J., 1st Lt. . . . . . . . . | Killed in Action | 23 Dec. '44 |

# HONOR ROLL

| NAME    RANK | TYPE CASUALTY | DATE |
|---|---|---|
| BALLARD, D. E., 1st Lt. . . . . . . . . . | Missing in Action | 25 Dec. '44 |
| HARGROVE, D. D., 2nd Lt. . . . . . . . | Missing in Action | 27 Dec. '44 |
| BALDWIN, E. C., Capt. . . . . . . . . . | Killed in Action | 29 Dec. '44 |
| PHELAN, J. W., 1st Lt. . . . . . . . . . | Missing in Action | 29 Dec. '44 |
| BARNARD, J. F., 2nd Lt. . . . . . . . . | Killed | 2 Jan. '45 |
| McFADDEN, J. J., 2nd Lt. . . . . . . . . | Missing in Action | 4 Jan. '45 |
| ROBERTSON, A., 2nd Lt. . . . . . . . . | Prisoner of War | 11 Jan. '45 |
| FAHLBERG, E. D., 1st Lt. . . . . . . . . | Rescued Partisans | 12 Jan. '45 |
| ROCK, E. S., 2nd Lt. . . . . . . . . . . | Killed in Action | 12 Jan. '45 |
| DOW, H. D., Major . . . . . . . . . . | Ret'd to Org. | 22 Jan. '45 |
| STRINGER, R. L., 2nd Lt. . . . . . . . . | Killed in Action | 25 Jan. '45 |
| GOMEZ, T. E., 2nd Lt. . . . . . . . . . | Killed in Action | 2 Feb. '45 |
| CLIFTON, K. E., 1st Lt. . . . . . . . . . | Killed in Action | 11 Feb. '45 |
| OZIMEK, E. J., 2nd Lt. . . . . . . . . . | Missing in Action | 11 Feb. '45 |
| FREEBORN, A. W., 2nd Lt. . . . . . . . | Missing in Action | 17 Feb. '45 |
| WALLING, E. L., 2nd Lt. . . . . . . . . | Missing in Action | 21 Feb. '45 |
| POWERS, J. E., 1st Lt. . . . . . . . . . | Killed in Action | 26 Feb. '45 |
| ASBURY, M. L., 1st Lt. . . . . . . . . . | Killed in Action | 27 Feb. '45 |
| SOUTHARD, J. C., 2nd Lt. . . . . . . . . | Killed in Action | 27 Feb. '45 |
| HAUSNER, S. E., 1st Lt. . . . . . . . . . | Ret'd to Org. | 3 Mar. '45 |
| LANGSTON, A. J., F/O . . . . . . . . . | Killed in Action | 7 Mar. '45 |
| MARTIN, L. F., 1st Lt. . . . . . . . . . | Missing in Action | 11 Mar. '45 |
| TRACY, L. E., 1st Lt. . . . . . . . . . . | Missing in Action | 14 Mar. '45 |
| MORRISON, W. F., 2nd Lt. . . . . . . . | Missing in Action | 19 Mar. '45 |
| MATTHEWS, A. M., 1st Lt. . . . . . . . | Rescued Partisans | 24 Mar. '45 |
| SCHLINDER, A. R., Major . . . . . . . . | Ret'd to Org. | 25 Mar. '45 |
| PARISH, G. L., 1st Lt. . . . . . . . . . | Killed in Action | 30 Mar. '45 |
| HUBBARD, N. K., 1st Lt. . . . . . . . . | Killed in Action | 3 Apr. '45 |
| SMITH, W. H., 1st Lt. . . . . . . . . . | Missing in Action | 3 Apr. '45 |
| STEWART, J. A., 2nd Lt. . . . . . . . . | Killed in Action | 9 Apr. '45 |
| BECK, J. M., 2nd Lt. . . . . . . . . . . | Ret'd to Org. | 10 Apr. '45 |
| SUMNER, W. W., 2nd Lt. . . . . . . . . | Missing in Action | 12 Apr. '45 |
| MILLER, W. R., F/O . . . . . . . . . . | Missing in Action | 15 Apr. '45 |
| POETON, R. R., 1st Lt. . . . . . . . . . | Killed in Action | 16 Apr. '45 |
| CLAYTON, R. H., 2nd Lt. . . . . . . . . | Killed in Action | 18 Apr. '45 |
| GORSKI, N. J., 1st Lt. . . . . . . . . . | Missing in Action | 18 Apr. '45 |
| WILKINSON, T., 2nd Lt. . . . . . . . . | Killed in Action | 19 Apr. '45 |
| PICKEREL, J. F., 1st Lt. . . . . . . . . | Ret'd to Org. | 19 Apr. '45 |
| PALMER, B. S., 1st Lt. . . . . . . . . . | Ret'd to Org. | 19 Apr. '45 |
| FISHER, G. M., 1st Lt. . . . . . . . . . | Missing in Action | 20 Apr. '45 |
| THOMPSON, R. C., 1st Lt. . . . . . . . . | Missing in Action | 20 Apr. '45 |
| ELLIS, R. C., 2nd Lt. . . . . . . . . . . | Ret'd to Org. | 20 Apr. '45 |
| SULZBACH, R. P., 2nd Lt. . . . . . . . . | Ret'd to Org. | 20 Apr. '45 |
| BACHMAN, A. A., 1st Lt. . . . . . . . . | Missing in Action | 22 Apr. '45 |
| BOETTCHER, R. E., 1st Lt. . . . . . . . | Ret'd to Org. | 22 Apr. '45 |
| GREGGERSON, R., 2nd Lt., . . . . . . . | Killed in Action | 22 Apr. '45 |
| PERRYMAN, C. R., 2nd Lt. . . . . . . . | Missing in Action | 22 Apr. '45 |
| McCLESKEY, R. L., F/O . . . . . . . . . | Missing in Action | 22 Apr. '45 |
| DOMIN, M. S., 1st Lt. . . . . . . . . . | Missing in Action | 23 Apr. '45 |
| KNIGHT, R. L., 2nd Lt. . . . . . . . . . | Killed in Action | 25 Apr. '45 |
| BADE, R. O., 1st Lt. . . . . . . . . . . | Ret'd to Org. | 25 Apr. '45 |
| BAGLEY, G. W., 1st Lt. . . . . . . . . . | Missing in Action | 28 Apr. '45 |
| VERME, S. J., 2nd Lt. . . . . . . . . . | Killed in Action | 29 Apr. '45 |
| GABOR, E. J., Major . . . . . . . . . . | Killed in Action | 1 May '45 |

*The Honor Roll is published, not as an official casualty list, but in tribute to, and in memory of, those officers whose devotion to duty carried with it the supreme sacrifice, or who suffered privation from long imprisonment, or lived the hunted life of an escapee. The list is entirely unofficial. It represents information which had been made known to the next of kin up to 2 May 1945.*

An old painting of Pisa in the 13th century when the 350th's headquarters was first erected.

The original design from which Palazzo Cavalieri was rebuilt in 1562. The tower has long since been torn down.

The last headquarters of the 350th Fighter Group was in sharp contrast to the tents and war-torn places it had always occupied. Known as the Scuola Normale Superiore, the building is the residence of the Higher University of Pisa, used in peace time for the libraries and housing of graduate students at the university.

This unusual building grew out of a medieval palace and seat of government which

Scuola Normale Superiore as occupied by the 350th Group headquarters in the late winter and spring of 1945.

United States, Brazilian, and Italian Colors in front of the Baptistry at the Cathedral, Pisa, before Military Mass.

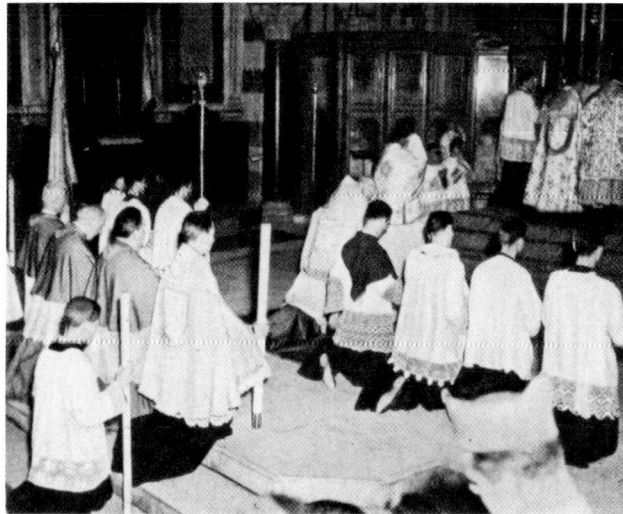

The Bishop of Pisa celebrates the Military Mass ordered by the President of the United States, May 1945.

was erected in 1286 A. D. In 1562 the palace was rebuilt by order of the Grand Duke of Tuscany and named « Palaza Cavalieri » (Knights' Palace) for the Military Order of the Pisan Knights. In 1932, the new wing was added and it became the property of the University of Pisa.

The magnificently frescoed facade of this building forms one side of the historic square on which the « Tower of Hunger », familiar in all children's story books, stood. The entrance to this tower (where Count Ugolino of Gherardesca, his son and nephews were imprisoned and starved to death) still leads into the arched « Palazzetto di Orologio » (Little Palace of the Clock).

In the headquarters building, the enlisted men's dayroom enjoyed the elaborately decorated ceiling of the original palace. Several of the Group Headquarters offices overlooked the historic square.

The Romanesque Cathedral and the Leaning Tower of Pisa.

The Arno River at Pisa, on which two billets were situated.

# COMMEMORATIVE DAYS

1 OCTOBER 1942. ORGANIZATION DAY. General Orders 6, Headquarters, VIII Fighter Command, Bushey Hall, Herts, England, dated 1 October 1942, stated « ...the following units having been constituted are hereby activated...: 350th Fighter Group, 345th Fighter Squadron, 346th Fighter Squadron, 347th Fighter Squadron ». This order was in compliance with a command of Major General Spaatz, 8th Air Force, 23 September 1942, pursuant to cable instructions signed « Marshall ». Based upon the date of activation established by the VIII Fighter Command, the Group Commander on 1 October 1943, Lt. Col. Ariel W. Nielsen, selected that date as the first annual Organization Day in accordance with AR 345-105, establishing a precedent which has since been followed. The first such anniversary was noted by posting the Commander's review upon bulletin boards, but otherwise could not be observed due to operational commitments. The second anniversary was observed by a similar published review, and an outdoor show by an Italian cast, presented after operations had ceased because of darkness.

★ ★ ★ ★ ★ ★

10 JULY 1943. INVASION OF SICILY. This date ended the most intensive 5 days of air defense patrols where the enemy was expected, flown by the 350th Fighter Group in the Mediterranean Campaign. Approximately 350 miles of sea lanes, over 110,000 ship miles of travel by 400 vessels, were given continual daylight protection. Included in the fleet were four battleships, one aircraft carrier, five cruisers, four minesweepers, sixty destroyers, many other naval units, troopships and cargo vessels which reached their destination — the stepping stone to Fortress Europe itself — without loss from aerial attack.

★ ★ ★ ★ ★ ★

6 APRIL 1944. « OPERATION STRANGLE ». The events of this date are fully described in the Battle Honor Citation on another page.

★ ★ ★ ★ ★ ★

23 DECEMBER 1944. NORTH APPENINES CAMPAIGN. By the end of the period beginning dawn, 23 December, ending noon 24 December, the 350th Fighter Group flying 21 missions of 121 sorties, destroyed 27 enemy aircraft and damaged 3; destroyed 12 enemy occupied buildings and damaged eleven; destroyed or immobilized 35 enemy transports, created 22 rail line cuts; rendered two rail bridges impassable; damaged 7 locomotives and 39 railroad cars, destroyed or damaged 6 pontoon barges and 2 river barges, devastated one enemy stores depot and disrupted one power station; silenced three enemy gun positions, and inflicted numerous personnel casualties upon the enemy. On this occasion the majority of all other Allied aircraft were held down by heavy overcasts. Facing the same conditions, the 350th Fighter Group flew all its requirements plus four flights made voluntarily.

★ ★ ★ ★ ★ ★

21 APRIL 1945. PO VALLEY CAMPAIGN. With solid clouds and heavy scud fog over its base so low that aircraft would have to take off on instruments, the 350th waited for clearing weather until 1600 hours in the hope of aiding Allied ground forces battling for Bologna. Between 1600 hours and 2030 hours, 46 aircraft took off voluntarily on an almost suicidal attempt to break through the solid mass of clouds which extended up to 7,000 feet with only the tops of the Appenines visible. The 350th aircraft, breaking through to the clear Po Valley, destroyed 105 motor trucks and damaged 63; immobilized 82 horse drawn Army vehicles; destroyed 4 Tiger tanks and 3 smaller tanks; destroyed and damaged 27 artillery pieces; fired 3 supply dumps; caused innumerable casualties and unreckoned damage by strafing columns of enemy troops and vehicle convoys; and sank one barge. Nine of our aircraft were hit by flak, and one was shot down, but the pilot evaded capture and escaped to our lines.